Water. Community Schools

BLOOM'S AND BEYOND
Higher Level Questions and Activities
for the Creative Classroom

Kay Davidson
Tressa Decker

© 2006 Pieces of Learning
CLC0392
ISBN 1-931334-84-6
Graphic Production by Sharolyn Hill
Cover design John Steele
www.piecesoflearning.com

Bloom's and Beyond
Higher Level Questions and Activities
for the Creative Classroom

Chapter 1

Introduction

Chapter 2

The Activities

Math

Social Studies

Science

Chapter 3

Creativity

Chapter 4

Assessment

Dedication

To Gary, Brennan and Brady....who inspire me, love me in spite of myself, and have helped me "bloom" in more ways than I can count.
To Momly, the best teacher, thinker, and believer I've known.
and
To my amazing colleagues at Concord and C.L.A.S.S. - who are some of the most creative people I know.   —Tressa

To my mom and dad, who always allowed me to think for myself
and
To my grandmother, who taught me the foundations of higher-level thinking by letting me play cards with the adults before I was even big enough to hold them all.   —Kay

A Word from the Authors

Dear Colleagues,

We have been known as the teachers with the classrooms that buzz with activity, where kids are actively engaged, moving full speed ahead with projects, research, and the acquisition of skills. We have been tagged as "creative" and "challenging" as we hold the highest expectations for our students. Colleagues have often asked how we do it. How do we maintain the level of activity, challenge, and student enthusiasm? The answer is both simple and complex.

We both firmly believe in challenging students to reach their fullest potentials – academically, physically, socially, and emotionally. Having students for six or more hours a day, we know that teachers play a major role in their successes. We have all observed classrooms where students are not being challenged, motivated, or engaged in learning. We want more for America's children. They deserve more! We want all teachers to understand what it means to take learning to a higher level and to have the tools to do just that. Out of that desire, the idea for this book emerged.

Reading Dr. Benjamin Bloom's original text, we found something quite different than the numerous, inconsistent lists of verbs that have been circulating for decades. What we uncovered was the pure, original message of Dr. Benjamin Bloom.

This "man before his time" truly wanted teachers to be able to comprehend the various levels of thinking and learning. His message is one of challenge and high expectations, encouraging teachers to spend time in the higher levels, because through the higher levels meaningful learning is achieved.

It is these levels that we have poured over – studying, discussing, pondering, and articulating the concepts actually penned by Bloom. We have not integrated our own interpretations; after all, we saw what years of "interpreting" did to the original Taxonomy. Rather, in this book, we share with you Bloom's original message, along with activities to help you boost your students to higher levels of thinking and achievement.

We hope you and your students will "bloom" as you take the challenge to move to the higher levels of the Taxonomy – where the creative and the passionate dwell.

Professionally yours,

Tressa and Kay

CHAPTER 1
INTRODUCTION

Dr. Benjamin Bloom
circa 1956

Bloom's Taxonomy: Some introspective comments. . .
Who knew?   There is no list of verbs in the original Taxonomy!

The Taxonomy of Educational Objectives, Handbook 1: Cognitive Domain, was originally proposed in the late 1940s with the intention of assisting college examiners with common assessment criteria. Dr. Benjamin Bloom, the leader of the project, also hoped that it might provide a means of communication within the field of education. Since its publication in 1956, the Taxonomy has not only accomplished Bloom's original goal but has remained a critical educational guide for student learning.

Bloom's Taxonomy, as it is so often called, wasn't written entirely by Dr. Benjamin Bloom. While the Taxonomy was Bloom's idea, it was written by a committee of more than 30 prominent educators from various universities. The Taxonomy in its entirety was divided into three main domains: the cognitive, the affective, and the psychomotor. Each domain was subsequently divided into subcategories, or chapters, to which different professors were assigned. Bloom's main responsibility in the cognitive domain was at the Knowledge and Evaluation levels, with much of the final detail work being done by his graduate assistant, David Krathwohl.

According to Bloom, education in the 1940s focused on the determination of which students had the ability to continue receiving advanced education and which were to be dropped at each stage of the educational process. The Taxonomy of Educational Objectives brought a structure to higher mental thought processes. In addition, however, it made educators aware that with the appropriate experiences and stimulation, student learning potential could be altered. Finally, research has shown that while focusing on higher levels in the classroom, lower-level skills are learned as a natural growth of the higher-level thinking process.

The Taxonomy didn't become popular over night. It wasn't until the 1960s that a need was seen to incorporate **behavioral** objectives not only in planning and evaluation, but in instruction as well. Prior to that time, delivering content was the major focus, with the level of **student behavior** never considered. However, due to criticism of standardized testing and the growing belief that most students could learn if given the appropriate educational experiences, a need for change in the classroom setting was eminent.

Suddenly learning environment and instructional approaches that relied on **student behavioral objectives** became the major educational focus. And while the Taxonomy's primary intention was to guide assessment, its logic and clarity caused educators to focus less on their delivery of instruction and more on student behavior. Awareness of the various levels of thinking also made it painfully obvious that as much as 90% of instructional time was frequently being spent at the Knowledge level.

Bloom's Taxonomy has changed the way educators think about the delivery of instruction. From a focus on student behavioral objectives to the incorporation of **academic standards** and the integration of many subjects into one lesson, the Taxonomy still stands strong. Why? Because there is still nothing else like it. While a few contemporary educators have made suggestions for improvement, Krathwohl notes that certain characteristics of the Taxonomy make it a steadfast necessity for those teachers who focus their method of instruction on student behavior:

- The major categories are easy to understand.
- Educational objectives and test items are plentiful.
- The hierarchical structure is scientifically respectable and easy to comprehend.
- The design of the framework and the vocabulary used was determined with teachers in mind.

Fifty years later, the Taxonomy is still highly respected and widely used as a guide to higher-level thinking. Charts with lists of verbs in each of the six levels make Bloom's Taxonomy a teacher-friendly resource for planning lessons and designing higher-level questions. But who knew? In our reading and study of the original Taxonomy, a list of verbs is nonexistent. That discovery was shocking . . . mind-jolting . . . startling . . . alarming . . . astonishing . . . surprising . . . amazing . . . astounding. So, as one might say after several rounds of "Telephone," where did all those Taxonomy verbs come from? It seems that each time someone took out a thesaurus, the verbs took on new meaning, and the lists got longer. . . and longer . . . and longer!

Thus, the following pages give a brief overview of each level of the Cognitive Domain with the **actual verbs** that are found in the Taxonomy's narrative. We've also provided data to show how the number of actual verbs has increased over the past 50 years.

With that in mind, we offer ***Bloom's and Beyond: Higher Level Questions and Activities for the Creative Classroom***. While we have exercised *some* academic freedom, we have made it our priority to bring teachers back to the original Taxonomy.

From the publisher . . .

It is our expectation **Bloom's and Beyond** will spark lively discussion. It is our hope that educators then examine their own lessons and determine if they are teaching to the higher levels of thinking and if students are genuinely learning at the higher levels.

If this book prompts you to examine the verbs and reflect on the questions, processes, and products you equate with teaching at the higher levels of the Taxonomy, our primary mission is accomplished. You have then yourself traveled through all 6 levels.

Lively debate among colleagues about our authors' research and their examples of verbs associated with their questions and activities will ultimately benefit all students.

DESCRIPTIONS AND VERBS IN THE TAXONOMY'S LOWER LEVELS OF THINKING

KNOWLEDGE: REMEMBER IT
Remember previously learned information.
Define basic terms.
Recall specific facts.

define	recognize
recall	remember

COMPREHENSION: INTERPRET IT
Understand the literal meaning of the information.
Interpret for later use.
Summarize in your own words.

conclude	explain	infer	rephrase
estimate	extend	interpret	summarize
	extrapolate	predict	translate
	generalize	reorder	
	use information		

APPLICATION: USE IT
Apply previously learned information in new situations.
Choose the correct method for problem solving.
Experiment to predict outcomes.

apply	experiment	solve
choose	predict	support
use	demonstrate	relate
	transfer	

DESCRIPTIONS AND VERBS IN THE TAXONOMY'S HIGHER LEVELS OF THINKING

ANALYSIS: TAKE IT APART
Break down information into understandable parts.
Recognize organizational structure.
Identify relationships and connections.

analyze
break down
clarify
classify

detect logical fallacies
discriminate
distinguish
identify technique
connect
identify motives

infer
recognize assumptions
recognize structure
relate

SYNTHESIS: CREATE IT
Create something new by making connections
with prior knowledge.
Develop a hypothesis or prediction.
Plan a procedure or a design.

arrange
combine
communicate
compose

create
design
discover
generalize

hypothesize
modify
perform
plan

produce
propose
write

EVALUATION: JUDGE IT
Assess for accuracy.
Evaluate based on a specific set of criteria.
Compare with the highest known standards.

assess
critique
evaluate

judge
locate errors
compare to highest
   standards

STATISTICS: VERB USAGE IN THE TAXONOMY

define
recall
recognize
remember

INTERPRETED AS. . .

collect

define
describe
draw

enumerate
examine

find

identify

know

label
list
locate

match
memorize

name

outline

read
recall
recite
recognize
record
relate
repeat
reproduce

select
show
state

tabulate
tell

(what
when
where
who)

write

All verbs listed were used
by at least 10% of the
sources checked.
An additional 39 verbs were
used by less than 10% and
eliminated.

Boldfaced verbs were
used by at least 50% of
the sources.

The verbs most used by
teachers were:

list	88%.
define	73%
name	68%
recall	63%

Verbs agreed upon by all
sources: 0%

K
N
O
W
L
E
D
G
E

STATISTICS: VERB USAGE IN THE TAXONOMY

conclude
estimate
explain
extend
extrapolate
generalize
infer
interpret
predict
reorder
rephrase
summarize
translate
use

COMPREHENSION

INTERPRETED AS. . .

classify
compare
contrast
convert

defend
demonstrate
describe
differentiate
discover
discuss
distinguish

estimate
explain
extend

generalize
give examples

identify
illustrate
infer
interpret

locate

outline

paraphrase
predict

recognize
report

restate
review

summarize
select

translate

understand

All verbs listed were used by at least 10% of the sources checked.
An additional 52 verbs were used by less than 10% and eliminated.

Boldfaced verbs were used by at least 50% of the sources.

The verbs most used by teachers were:

explain	70%
describe	58%
summarize	55%
interpret	53%

Verbs agreed upon by all sources: 0%

STATISTICS: VERB USAGE IN THE TAXONOMY

apply
choose
demonstrate
experiment
predict
relate
solve
support
transfer
use

INTERPRETED AS. . .

apply

calculate
change
choose
classify
complete
compute
construct

demonstrate
determine
develop
discover
dramatize

employ
examine
experiment

illustrate
implement
interpret
interview

manipulate
modify
operate

predict
prepare
produce

relate

schedule
show
sketch
solve

transfer

use

write

All verbs listed were used by at least 10% of the sources checked.
An additional 60 verbs were used by less than 10% and eliminated.

Boldfaced verbs were used by at least 50% of the sources.

The verbs most used by teachers were:

apply	70%.
use	70%
solve	65%
demonstrate	55%

Verbs agreed upon by all sources: 0%

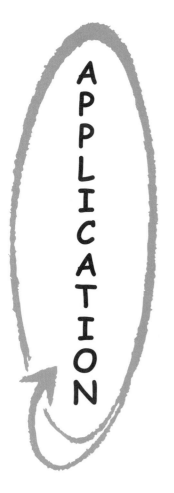

A
P
P
L
I
C
A
T
I
O
N

STATISTICS: VERB USAGE IN THE TAXONOMY

analyze
break down
clarify
classify
connect
discriminate
distinguish
infer
relate

also:
detect logical fallacies
identify motives
identify technique
recognize assumptions
recognize structure

A
N
A
L
Y
S
I
S

INTERPRETED AS. . .

analyze
appraise
arrange
assume

break down

calculate
categorize
classify
compare
conclude
contrast
criticize

deconstruct
deduce
determine
diagnose
diagram
differentiate
discriminate
discover
dissect
distinguish

examine
experiment
explain

generalize

identify
illustrate
infer
inspect
investigate

order
organize
outline

point out

question

relate

separate
subdivide
survey

test

All verbs listed were used by at least 10% of the sources checked.
An additional 44 verbs were used by less than 10% and eliminated.

Boldfaced verbs were used by at least 50% of the sources.

The verbs most used by teachers were:

compare	65%.
analyze	60%
distinguish	53%
contrast	50%

Verbs agreed upon by all sources: 0%

STATISTICS: VERB USAGE IN THE TAXONOMY

arrange
combine
communicate
compose
create
design
discover
generalize
hypothesize
perform
plan
produce
propose
write

INTERPRETED AS. . .

arrange
assemble

categorize
combine
compare
compile
compose
concoct
construct
contrast
create

deduce
design
develop
devise
discuss

formulate

generalize
generate

hypothesize

imagine
integrate
invent

make
manage
modify

organize
originate

plan
predict

prepare
present
pretend
produce
propose

rearrange
reconstruct
reinforce
relate
reorganize
revise
rewrite

set up

write

All verbs listed were used by at least 10% of the sources checked.
An additional 49 verbs were used by less than 10% and eliminated.

Boldfaced verbs were used by at least 50% of the sources.

The verbs most used by teachers were:

create	73%
design	78%
plan	60%
formulate	43%

Verbs agreed upon by all sources: 0%

S Y N T H E S I S

STATISTICS: VERB USAGE IN THE TAXONOMY

assess
critique
evaluate
judge
locate errors

also:
compare to highest
standard

INTERPRETED AS. . .

appraise
argue
assess

choose
compare
conclude
contrast
convince
criticize
critique

debate
decide
deduce
defend
describe
determine
discriminate

estimate
evaluate
explain

give an opinion
grade

interpret

judge
justify

predict
prioritize

rank
rate
recommend

select
summarize
support

test

value

All verbs listed were used by at least 10% of the sources checked.
An additional 48 verbs were used by less than 10% and eliminated.

Boldfaced verbs were used by at least 50% of the sources.

The verbs most used by teachers were:
> judge   88%.
> evaluate   55%

Verbs agreed upon by all sources: 0%

E
V
A
L
U
A
T
I
O
N

KNOWLEDGE: REMEMBER IT!

Remember previously learned information.
Define basic terms.
Recall specific facts.

Definition *remembering an idea or fact in a form very close to that in which it was originally encountered.* Realizing that **knowing** may involve more complex thought processes such as relating, reorganizing, and using judgment, Knowledge is basically information that is stored in the brain. The ability to recall or remember that information in its original form is **Knowledge**, the lowest level of thinking.

Subcategories at the Knowledge level include Knowledge of Specifics, Knowledge of Ways of Dealing with Specifics, and Knowledge of Universals. Examples include: knowledge of terms, specific facts (including dates and events), methods of organizing, common practices, judgment criteria, and rules of social behavior.

Knowledge differs from the other five categories in that **remembering** is the major psychological process. In the other categories remembering is only one small part of a more complex process of thinking.

Highest level: remembering the theory of relativity or evolution

COMMONLY USED VERBS AT THE KNOWLEDGE LEVEL:

| **define** | label | name | **recognize** | state |
| describe | list | **recall** | **remember** | |

*(Actual verbs from the Taxonomy are **bold**.)*

Lowest level: naming the capital that matches a particular state

> *Remember: At the Knowledge level,*
> *students recall previously learned information.*

TWENTY QUESTIONS / PROMPTS FOR YOUR STUDENTS

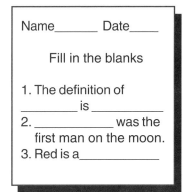

1. What is a kudo? *define*
2. How is Congress organized? *remember*
3. What is the law of gravity? *define*
4. Name the four seasons. *remember*
5. What is photosynthesis? *define*
6. Which state on the map is Indiana? *recognize*
7. How many donuts are in a dozen? *recall*
8. What is the theory of evolution? *define*
9. Which state has the largest area? *recall*
10. Where is the Table of Contents located? *remember*
11. Who was the first president of the United States? *recall*
12. What type of punctuation is needed in this sentence? *remember*
13. Give three definitions for the word *bank*. *define*
14. Underline the word that best fits the picture. *define*
15. What is the correct way to set a table? *recall*
16. When was John F. Kennedy assassinated? *recall*
17. List the primary colors. *remember*
18. What type of clothing was typically worn during the 1700s? *remember*
19. List the five major categories of vertebrates. *remember*
20. What information do you need to determine this food's nutritional value? *recall*

SAMPLE PRODUCTS AND ACTIVITIES AT THE KNOWLEDGE LEVEL

fill-in-the blank worksheet	words/definitions	basic fact worksheet
premade, labeled map	spelling list	matching worksheet
fact file	labeled diagram	observation
true/false quizzes	study cards	discussions
multiple choice worksheets	"Concentration" games	spelling test question/
list of story elements	list of writing ideas	answer

Classroom activities at the Knowledge level ask students to . . . recall information, make lists, label maps, memorize facts, and answer right/wrong questions.

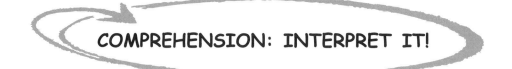

COMPREHENSION: INTERPRET IT!

Understand the literal meaning of the information.
Interpret for later use.
Summarize in your own words.

Definition *to know what is being communicated and to be able to make use of the information.* The communication may be verbal, pictorial, symbolic, or experiential. It is not meant to be synonymous with complete understanding or having a full grasp of the message — just its **literal content**. Comprehension is the lowest level of **understanding** but is probably the most emphasized in classroom instruction.

There are basically three **types** of comprehension:

translation: to put in another language, other terms, or another usable form

interpretation: to reorder or classify the ideas so that inferences, generalizations, or summaries can be made

extrapolation: to make estimates or predictions based on what is given in the communication

Comprehension is different from Analysis because it **interprets literal meaning** only. At the Analysis level, more inference and recognition of *unstated* assumptions impacts thinking.

Highest level: predicting continuation of trends based on information read

COMMONLY USED VERBS AT THE COMPREHENSION LEVEL

classify	explain	predict	summarize
conclude	generalize	reorder	translate
estimate	interpret	rephrase	understand
			use

*(Actual verbs from the Taxonomy are **bold**.)*

Lowest level: being able to summarize a story

Remember: At the Comprehension level, students interpret literal meaning.

TWENTY QUESTIONS / PROMPTS FOR YOUR STUDENTS

1. What is the main idea of this paragraph? *generalize*
2. Which details support the topic sentence? *explain*
3. What does this cartoon portray? *interpret*
4. Can you use this word in a sentence? *use*
5. Can you retell the story in your own words? *summarize*

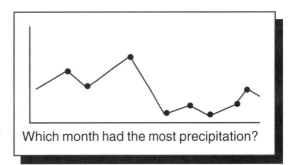

Which month had the most precipitation?

6. What was the writer trying to say in this poem? *interpret*
7. What do you think uno, dos, tres . . . means? *translate*
8. What message is this infomercial communicating? *interpret*
9. Use the graph to answer the following questions. *use*
10. From three examples, choose the best definition for this word. *understand*
11. In your own words, summarize what the mayor said in his speech. *summarize*
12. What symbols might you use to represent landmarks on this map? *translate*
13. Which graph illustrates the information needed to solve this problem? *interpret*
14. Can you summarize the points of view presented in the debate? *summarize*
15. Can you estimate how many copies of this book have been sold? *estimate*
16. Why did the United States become its own country? *generalize*
17. Based on the data in this table, which of the following is true? *interpret*
18. What do you think the author means when he says ____? *interpret*
19. Why do you think these two characters are such good friends? *infer*
20. Do you have enough information to answer the question? *conclude*

SAMPLE PRODUCTS AND ACTIVITIES AT THE COMPREHENSION LEVEL

book report	word problems	annotated bibliography
blueprint	study sheet	pattern/instructions
ESL activities	book summary	questions from a chart
experiment notes	storytelling	questions from a graph
collage	dramatization	speech overview
test review	music reading	graph representations
English translation	poetry interpretation	math computation

> *Classroom activities at the Comprehension level ask students to . . . translate and interpret information so that they can use it.*

APPLICATION: USE IT!

Apply previously learned information to new situations.
Choose the correct method for problem solving.
Experiment to predict outcomes.

Definition *given a problem new to the student, he will apply what he knows and use it in this situation without being prompted.* The student might use general ideas, procedures, or methods that he has remembered and apply them to this new situation. This transfer of training happens more readily when the student has learned methods for attacking problems, can state generalizations, and has developed self-confidence and control. Because the student will apply and predict, teaching objectives at this level sound very much alike.

The difference between Application and Comprehension is that at the Comprehension level, the student understands the literal message or the abstraction well enough to verbalize or demonstrate it when asked to do so. At the Application level, however, that understanding is actively put to use while **solving a new problem — without being prompted** — and without strategies to choose from.

Highest level: setting up a procedure for solving a problem

COMMONLY USED VERBS AT THE APPLICATION LEVEL:

apply	**demonstrate**	**predict**	**support** a conclusion
choose	discover	**relate**	**transfer** of training
calculate	**experiment**	**solve**	**use**

*(Actual verbs found in the Taxonomy are **bold**.)*

Lowest level: supporting a conclusion with evidence

> *Remember: At the Application level, students apply what they already know to new situations.*

TWENTY QUESTIONS/PROMPTS FOR YOUR STUDENTS

1. Why did you choose this answer? *support*
2. Why won't this light come on? *solve*
3. How are these two related? *relate*
4. What do you think will happen? *predict*
5. How is multiplication like addition? *relate*
6. What reasons support your conclusion? *support*
7. How will you make use of this information? *use*
8. What questions will you ask in the interview? *choose*
9. Can you draw a flow chart showing your problem solving steps? *calculate*
10. Why do you think this piece of wood will float? *predict*
11. What materials will you need to prepare for this lab? *solve*
12. How can you figure out the area of this triangle? *choose the correct method*
13. How will you teach this math concept to a friend? *transfer*
14. Can you make a chart to show how many books you have read? *apply*
15. Can you transfer the grammar rules into your story writing? *transfer*
16. How does the Law of Gravity explain the outcome of this experiment? *support*
17. Find the area of the classroom. *use*
18. According to the definition of <u>extinct</u>, which animals would fall into this category? *relate*
19. What information is needed before you can answer this story problem? *solve*
20. What would happen if we skipped lunch every day this week? *predict*

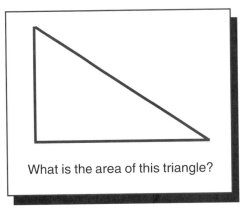

What is the area of this triangle?

SAMPLE PRODUCTS AND ACTIVITIES AT THE APPLICATION LEVEL

board game	computer simulation	experiment	map making
chart	diagram	illustration	model construction
collection	display	interview	peer teaching
			problem solving

> *Classroom activities at the Application level ask students to . . . solve problems by applying what they know to a new situation.*

ANALYSIS: TAKE IT APART!

Break down information into understandable parts.
Recognize organizational structure.
Identify relationships and connections.

Definition *the breakdown of a communication for the purpose of clarification.* This occurs when students are able to recognize how the information is organized as well as recognize the technique used to convey the message. The hierarchy and relationships between ideas are made explicit. The ability to recognize unstated assumptions is a major part of analysis as well as the ability to distinguish important from less important information.

Analysis differs from Comprehension and Application in the following ways:
At the Comprehension level, the emphasis is on understanding the literal meaning.
At the Application level, the understanding of a generalization or principle is applied to a new situation.
At the Analysis level, the material is **broken down into parts for the purpose of determining relationships and organizational patterns.**

Highest level: identifying relationships and connections between pieces of information

COMMONLY USED VERBS AT THE ANALYSIS LEVEL:

analyze	compare	**discriminate**	**recognize structure**
break down	**connect**	**distinguish**	**relate**
classify	contrast	**infer**	separate

*(Actual verbs from the Taxonomy are **bold**.)*

Lowest level: recognizing the organizational structure of the information

> **Remember: At the Analysis level, students break down situations or quantities of information into smaller, understandable parts.**

TWENTY QUESTIONS/PROMPTS FOR YOUR STUDENTS:

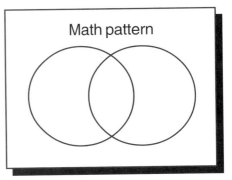

1. Is this statement a fact or opinion? *distinguish*
2. What do you read between the lines? *infer*
3. Why is this information relevant? *analyze*
4. How is this information arranged? *recognize structure*
5. What caused this outcome? *identify technique*
6. What can you infer from your observation? *infer*
7. What assumptions did you have to make? *recognize assumptions*
8. What is the general structure of this story? *recognize structure*
9. How would you break down this story into chapters? *break down*
10. How will you distinguish fact from hypothesis? *distinguish*
11. What was the author's purpose for writing this chapter? *infer*
12. What do you question about this theory? *detect logical fallacies*
13. How should we organize this information? *classify*
14. What pattern do you see in this group of numbers? *recognize structure*
15. What is the major premise behind your argument? *identify motives*
16. What main question is the author trying to answer in this chapter? *distinguish*
17. What is the relationship between these two ideas? *relate*
18. What technique is being used in this persuasive speech? *identify technique*
19. What information contributed to your being able to solve the mystery? *analyze*
20. Is this a logical explanation? (Does it make sense?) *detect logical fallacies*

SAMPLE PRODUCTS AND ACTIVITIES AT THE ANALYSIS LEVEL

analysis of artwork
cause-effect
crossword puzzle
dissecting plants/animals

family tree
main idea-detail
mobile display
outlining

scientific observation
sentence diagramming
survey
word sorting

Classroom activities at the Analysis level ask students to . . . find patterns, ask questions, make inferences from observations, and separate important from unimportant information.

SYNTHESIS: CREATE IT!

Create something new by making connections with prior knowledge.
Develop a hypothesis or prediction.
Plan a procedure or a design.

Definition *the putting together of elements and parts to form a whole.* This unique arrangement must create a new pattern or structure that was clearly not there before. This level of the Taxonomy clearly recognizes creative behavior. However, the creative expression must be within the limits of the problems and/or materials being worked with. Synthesis does not imply free creative expression.

The three **subcategories** of Synthesis include the production of:
- a unique communication such as a creative essay or an extemporaneous speech.
- a plan that proposes ways of testing a hypothesis, that integrates results to form a new conclusion, or that conveys a unique design.
- abstract relations such as the formulation of new theories, ideas, or discoveries.

Synthesis is different from comprehension in that the ideas that are gathered are new. Comprehension, Application, and Analysis also connect elements and construct meaning, but the results are less focused on originality and uniqueness. In Synthesis alone the student must draw upon elements from many sources to **produce a structure or pattern that clearly was not there before.**

Highest level: designing a new chemical process based on what is known about chemistry, unit operations, and technology

COMMONLY USED VERBS AT THE SYNTHESIS LEVEL:

arrange	**create**	generalize	**modify**
combine	**design**	**hypothesize**	**plan**
compose	develop	invent	write

*(Actual verbs from the Taxonomy are **bold**.)*

Lowest level: create a list of new ways to use this object

> *Remember: At the Synthesis level, ideas are rearranged to form a new whole, clearly unlike what was there before.*

TWENTY QUESTIONS/PROMPTS FOR YOUR STUDENTS

1. How will you express that idea in writing? *write*
2. How will you test your hypothesis? *hypothesize*
3. How do you propose to organize this project? *organize*
4. Compose a song about this event. *compose*
5. What would happen if . . ? *hypothesize*
6. How would you turn this poem into a song? *modify*
7. Can you design a tool that will make this job easier? *design*
8. How will you combine these elements to make something new? *combine*
9. Using this set of objects, what invention can you create? *invent*
10. What new discoveries can you come up with by using this theory? *discover*
11. Will you stand up and make a few brief comments about your idea? *generalize*
12. If you take new ideas into consideration, how might your original thoughts change? *combine*
13. How many new uses can you think of for this object? *develop*
14. How many ways can you think of to solve this problem? *hypothesize*
15. Given these specifications, how would you design a new school cafeteria? *design*
16. Propose a plan for lowering taxes in the United States. *propose*
17. How can you rewrite this story to make it more descriptive? *modify*
18. What solution would you suggest? *propose*
19. What kind of puzzle can you create using this week's spelling words? *create*
20. Write a mystery combining the characters from these two books. *combine*

New uses for a . . .
Song

Invention Design

SAMPLE PRODUCTS AND ACTIVITIES AT THE SYNTHESIS LEVEL

advertisement	design for a tool	journal narrative
art gallery	design of a process	illustrated original story
comic strip	extemporaneous speech	musical review
creative writing	group mural	poetry writing

Classroom activities at the Synthesis level ask students to . . . design a plan, write an original communication, or create something new.

EVALUATION: JUDGE IT!

Assess for accuracy.
Evaluate based on a specific set of criteria.
Compare with the highest known standards.

Definition *judging the value of ideas, works, solutions, methods, or materials for a purpose.* A set of specific criteria as well as standards are used in the appraisal. While evaluation is the "last stage" of the Taxonomy, it is not necessarily the last step in thinking or problem solving. It is placed at level six because the process of Evaluation involves all the other behaviors: Knowledge, Comprehension, Application, Analysis, and Synthesis.

Evaluation is divided into **two types** of judgments:
Internal: locating errors within the work being evaluated
External: evaluating the work based on a specific means-ends relationship; given the end product, how appropriate and correct was the means?

Evaluation is different from Analysis in that **a final judgment is made** after Knowledge has been Applied and Analysis has been completed.

Highest level: determining which essay best conveys the spirit of freedom and independence

COMMONLY USED VERBS AT THE EVALUATION LEVEL:

appraise	conclude	**evaluate**	justify
assess	critique	give an opinion	locate errors
compare	**defend**	**judge**	recommend

*(Actual verbs from the Taxonomy are **bold**.)*

Lowest level: locating errors in content or logical thinking

Remember: At the Evaluation level, students are asked to judge something based on a distinct set of criteria.

TWENTY QUESTIONS/PROMPTS FOR YOUR STUDENTS

1. Which one is the best? *compare*
2. What is the most important? *value*
3. What do you think about this issue? *appraise*
4. Is this story well written? *judge*
5. How would you assess this project? *assess*
6. Why is this your favorite? *critique*
7. Are these sentences written correctly? *locate errors*
8. Why is this problem so difficult? *criticize*
9. Can you find errors in logic for this hypothesis? *locate errors*
10. What set of criteria would best judge these science fair projects? *appraise*
11. Does the method used in solving this problem deserve full credit? *value*
12. Write your thoughts and opinions about this topic. *critique*
13. What criteria would you use to assess this product? *assess*
14. Arrange this list of people in the order of their importance. *value*
15. Evaluate the difficulty level of this problem. *evaluate*
16. Give your opinion of the speech based on the rubric criterion. *judge*
17. Why is this painting more valuable than others? *value*
18. Why doesn't this answer make sense? *locate errors*
19. If your house were on fire, what objects would you save? *value*
20. Do the arguments presented in this speech relate to the conclusion? *compare*

Science Fair

The Effects of Global Warming

SAMPLE PRODUCTS AND ACTIVITIES AT THE EVALUATION LEVEL

letter to the editor	editorial	panel discussion
mock trial	self evaluations	revision
peer feedback	proofreading	product judging
poetry evaluation	grading papers	music critiquing
art critiquing	item appraisal	criteria design

Classroom activities at the Evaluation level ask students to . . . make recommendations, assess value, critique ideas, make choices, and support opinions.

CHAPTER 2
THE ACTIVITIES

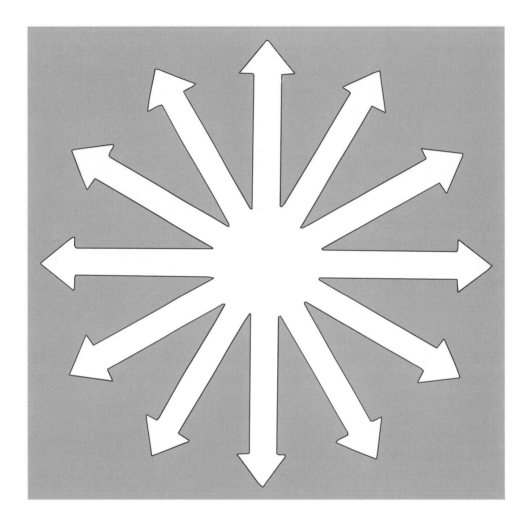

The Activities

The following pages are filled with a variety of activities designed to engage, motivate, and challenge students. Each activity is clearly planned out, and questions and prompts are provided for each of Bloom's levels. Your differentiation has been done for you! Remember, the challenge to you is to move to the higher levels with your students. Bloom himself recommended this! He knew that through higher-level thinking, processing, and problem solving, students would naturally work through the lower levels.

So, here you go . . . onward, upward, and BEYOND!

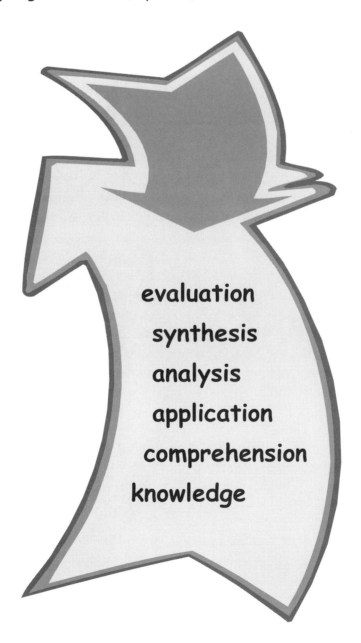

evaluation

synthesis

analysis

application

comprehension

knowledge

Language Arts

BOOK TALK

Activity
Overview: After reading a book, the student prepares a 2-3 minute "book talk" to persuade classmates to either read or avoid this book.

Materials: copy of book, various presentation materials needed (this will vary, depending on the type of presentation each student chooses to make)

Lead In: Explain to students the purpose of a book talk: *to give other readers your opinion about the book, supported by examples and persuasive techniques.*
Demonstrate an "exemplar" book talk – either by doing one yourself or showing a videotape of a student from a previous class.
Instruct about various persuasive techniques and oral presentation skills.

Give students a time frame and final due date, along with criteria for a booktalk and other requirements that you want submitted.

Procedure: Students read a book of their choice.
A time is scheduled for each student to present their "book talk" to the class.
Students make their 2-3 minute "book talk" presentations.
Option: have the class critique each "book talk" for effectiveness.

Lower Level Questions/Prompts for Literal Comprehension:
K -   What was the title of the book? Was the book fiction or nonfiction? *name/recall*
C -   What kind of audience would enjoy reading this book? *predict*
Ap - Where would this book be shelved in the library? *transfer*

Higher Level Questions/Prompts for Reflective Response:
An - List one important event from the beginning, middle, and end of the book. *recognize structure/break down*
S -   Create a new title for this book. Why would you choose that new title? *create*
E -   Judge the overall quality of the book. Did you find any problems or errors in the book? *locate errors*

 WORD SORTS

Activity
Overview: Students practice their spelling words by sorting them in
             various ways.

Materials: spelling words on 1" x 3" inch strips of paper
             a snack-sized zippered bag

Lead In: The teacher will show students various ways in which they may sort
             words. Some examples may include by vowel sound, number of
             syllables, part of speech, or classification.

Procedure: Students will work in small groups or pairs to sort words in as many
             ways as they can. Words may or may not be written on a word sort
             chart.
             Students will put words back in their zippered bag to use again the
             next day.

Lower Level Questions/Prompts:
K-   Write each one of this week's spelling words on a 1" x 3" strip of
     paper. *remember*
C-   Describe the spelling pattern for long vowel words. *describe*
Ap- How can you apply what you know about phonics to sort these
     words? *apply*

Higher Level Questions/Prompts:
An- Sort these words in a new way. *classify*
S-   Did you discover any generalizations about these words?
     generalize
E-   Judge how this activity has helped you to learn your spelling
     words. *judge*

BOOK CHAT

Activity Overview: Book Chat is a relaxed, conversational-style discussion about the text. It is designed for a small reading group (<10 students).

Materials: each student brings a copy of the text (i.e. picture book) student Reading Log or Journal with any notes about the text

Lead In: Book Chats can be done after the text has been read. Students should have completed the assigned reading so they are prepared to discuss the text at this Book Chat. Have students sit in a circle, or around a table, so everyone can make eye contact.

Procedure: One person gets things started with a lead off-question. (knowledge level) Everyone participates by answering a question directed at them. More than one person may respond to a question (this is highly encouraged at the higher levels to broaden the perspective). Students do not have to raise their hands to speak, but should practice good manners by not interrupting, sharing the floor, and using active listening skills.

Lower Level Questions/Prompts for Literal Comprehension:
K - What genre is this book? Who is the author? Who is the illustrator? *recall*
C - Summarize the events in the story. *summarize*
Ap - Use an example from the book to help us understand what the main character was like. *Support*

Higher Level Questions/Prompts for Reflective Response:
An - How are you like/unlike the main character? Give an example or two. *compare*
S - What could be a different ending for this story? *modify*
E - Would you recommend this book to another class to read? Why or why not? *recommend*

Activity
Overview: Students bring in one or two favorite recipes from home. Then, students create original recipes which are compiled, along with the "real" family recipes, into a class recipe book.

Materials: ingredients for a simple recipe, pencils, crayons, and paper

Lead In: Give students 2-3 days to bring in their recipes from home. Collect and type for publication in the recipe book.
Following instruction on measurement in Math, actually make a batch of cookies or a cake from scratch, using measurement tools in the kitchen (measuring cups and spoons, etc.)
Now that everyone has had the experience of following a recipe, they are ready to create original ones on their own.

Procedure: Students write an original recipe, using measurements for each ingredient, followed by directions for cooking...encourage creativity!
Students write a final copy and draw a picture of their food creation.
The teacher will photocopy the students' handwritten and hand-drawn recipes and insert them into the class recipe book.
After the recipe book is compiled, copied, and distributed to the class, give students a chance to read through it. Read it together, silently, with a partner, or other way so students become familiar with the recipes included.
You may even want to try one of the recipes in class!
Then, you are ready to process the learning with the following questions:

Lower Level Questions/Prompts:
K - List three different recipes that use tablespoon as a measurement. *list*
C - Explain the format of each recipe. (ingredients, method) *explain*
Ap - Demonstrate how to accurately measure using measuring spoons. *demonstrate*

Higher Level Questions/Prompts:
An - Classify the recipes according to difficulty, using various categories. *classify*
S - If you were going to design a one-of-a-kind recipe book, what would it be like? What would you include in it? How would it be different? *design*
E - Make a list of five recipes you'd recommend from our class recipe book. *recommend*

CONVINCE ME!

Activity
Overview: Students write a persuasive letter to a real person, using correct form and technique, and then mail the letter via the United States Postal Service.

Materials: paper, pencil, envelopes, stamps (may ask students to provide)

Lead In: Teacher instructs on how to write a persuasive letter, correct letter format, and envelope format.
Generate a list of persuasive words and post the list in the classroom.
The class goes over current issues about which they have opinions.
Students choose one issue that they would like to persuade someone to take action on. (i.e. no more school on Fridays, save the park by the school, let us have soda pop for lunch, we should help the hurricane survivors).
Students identify to whom they will be writing their persuasive letter.

Procedure: Students write persuasive letters.
Students address the envelopes and mail them.
Students predict whether they think they will get responses to their letters. What effect will their letters have on the issues?
As responses come in the mail, students are able to share them with the class by reading aloud and then posting the replies on a bulletin board for all to see.

Lower Level Questions/Prompts:
K -   What is the issue about which you are trying to persuade someone? *remember*
C -   Tell us your stand on the issue. What do you want to see happen? *explain*
Ap - What will happen if nothing is changed about your issue? *predict*

Higher Level Questions/Prompts:
An - How is a persuasive letter similar to/different than a friendly letter? *compare*
S -   What would be a catchy slogan for your stance on this issue? Create one. *create*
E -   Why is this issue so important? *appraise*

Activity
Overview: After a read-aloud, students will focus on reflection and analysis rather
             than literal comprehension. Do they still wonder about anything after
             hearing the story?

Materials: picture book
             pencils, response journals

Lead In: The teacher will have written "I wonder..." on the board prior to
             reading.
             Students will sit on the floor as the teacher reads a picture book to
             the class.
             Students will have their reading response journals on their desks or
             in their laps for note-taking purposes.

Procedure: The teacher will introduce the book and help students to make text to
             self connections before beginning.
             The teacher will ask some questions before starting the story so
             students have a purpose for listening.
             After reading, the students will discuss the story.
             They will then write about something they are still wondering about
             after reading.

Lower Level Questions/Prompts for Literal Comprehension:
K - Where does this story take place? *remember*
C - What is the main idea of this story? *summarize*
Ap- How was the mystery solved? *calculate*

Higher Level Questions/Prompts for Reflective Response:
An- How does this book compare with the book we read yesterday?
     compare
S - What additional character could you create to add to the story?
     modify
E - Why would you read this book again? *justify*

Activity Overview: *You're the Teacher*™ is an editing program designed to help students catch errors in capitalization, punctuation, and spelling.

Set Up: *You're the Teacher*™ editing sheets (available Gr. 1-8; see Resources) a red pen for each student

Lead In: mini-lessons during the week to introduce or review mechanics/conventions skills in that level's academic standards

Procedure: Each Friday, students will have the opportunity to work individually or in pairs to find errors in sentences, letters, or paragraphs.
They will put three lines under capitalization errors, insert missing punctuation, and correct the spelling errors.

Lower Level Questions/Prompts:
K - Can you remember how many errors you need to find? *remember*
C - Summarize the main skill(s) being focused on in this week's *You're the Teacher*™. *summarize*
Ap - Apply what you know about rules for commas as you correct the punctuation. *use*

Higher Level Questions/Prompts:
An - Break down the errors into three types. *break down*
S - Rewrite the first sentence to create a clearer vision. *modify*
E - Critique this week's *You're the Teacher*™ in terms of its difficulty level. *critique*

Activity
Overview: In partner reading, all pairs of students read quietly at the same time in the classroom. Students should choose a book they are interested in reading.

Set Up: copy of a story for each student or pair (from basal, picture book, periodical, etc.)
a quiet, well-lit place on the floor or at a table or desk

Lead In: Students will review behavioral expectations for reading together. Students will be responsible for choosing their own partners and books they will read together.

Procedure: The two students will read the story aloud, alternating pages.
The listener must ask a question at the end of each page that the reader will answer or the two will discuss.
Students alternate roles after each page.
After reading, the students will fill out a recommendation card to put on the class bulletin board.

Lower Level Questions/Prompts for Literal Comprehension:
K - Can you recall the names of the characters? *recall*
C - Can you summarize the story up to this point? *summarize*
Ap- Use the strategy of *rereading* to find an example of figurative language. *use*

Higher Level Questions/Prompts for Reflective Response:
An- Can you relate this story to a personal life experience? *relate*
S - Can you work together to produce another ending to this story? *write*
E - After critiquing this book, do you recommend it to your friends? Why or why not? *recommend*

Activity Overview: Readers' Circle is a relaxed, conversational-style discussion about the text. It is designed for a small reading group (<10 students).

Materials: each student brings a copy of the assigned text (i.e. novel, poem)
student Reading Log or Journal with any notes about the text

Lead In: Readers' Circle can be held after the text has been read, after each chapter, or after every few chapters have been read…whatever works for your classroom.
Students should have completed the assigned reading so they are prepared to discuss that portion of the text at this Readers' Circle.
Have students sit in a circle, so everyone can make eye contact

Procedure: One person gets things started with a lead off-question
Everyone participates by answering a question directed at them
More than one person may respond to a question (this is highly encouraged at the higher levels to broaden the perspective)
Students do not have to raise their hand to speak, but should practice good manners by not interrupting, sharing the floor, and using active listening skills.

Lower Level Questions/Prompts for Literal Comprehension:
K - Name the main character(s) in the story. *name*
C - Summarize the events in the story. *summarize*
Ap - Use an example of descriptive language to illustrate the setting of this story. *support/use*

Higher Level Questions/Prompts for Reflective Response:
An - What distinguishes this book from other novels you have read? *distinguish*
S - Write the sequel to this book. Plan the events and changes in characters. *plan*
E - Critique the author's use of slang in this novel. *critique*
Why should/shouldn't other students read this book? *justify*
What was the author's best technique or story idea in this book? *give an opinion*

OWNER'S MANUAL

Activity Overview: Students create an owner's manual for any product or task. This requires them to think through a systematic, how-to explanation of something.

Materials: boxes/packages from various products (pool float, kite, game, phone, DVD, assemble-yourself furniture, etc.), pencil, paper

Lead In: Prior to this activity, students have had the opportunity to read various owner's manuals for various products. A list is made of things to include in an owner's manual.
The teacher instructs about logical order in writing a how-to procedure.
Templates or specific format requirements are given.

Procedure: Students choose the product for which they will create the owner's manual.
Using the list of "things to include in an owner's manual," students will write their own manual.
Illustrations, diagrams, and tables may be included, especially if students are struggling to put things into words.
Students share their owner's manuals with each other.

Lower Level Questions/Prompts:
K - Recall at least three different sections included in most owners' manuals. *recall*
C - Why is it important to read manuals carefully? *conclude*
Ap - Experiment by following an owner's manual procedure exactly as it reads, then do it again, but change or omit one of the steps. What happens when you change it? *experiment*

Higher Level Questions/Prompts:
An - What are the most commonly used commands in owner's manuals? *analyze*
S - Can you develop a better format for an owner's manual? What would you include? *develop*
E - How can a company judge the effectiveness of its owner's manuals? Judge the effectiveness of the manual you created. *judge*

Activity
Overview: After reading several assigned chapters in a class novel, students will
focus on reflection and analysis rather than literal comprehension.

Materials: copy of the book for each student
optional sticky notes to mark pages and writing journals for note
taking
transparency, handout, or PowerPoint® slides that present higher-level
questions

Lead In: The teacher will engage students in discussion about the book and encourage students to make text-to-self connections.
Reflective answers will be modeled and discussed.
The teacher will ask higher level questions before students start reading
the next section so they have a purpose for reading.

Procedure: After reading, the students will discuss the story and respond to one or
more higher level questions in their journals.
Teacher and student responses will be shared and discussed the next
day.

Lower Level Questions/Prompts for Literal Comprehension:
K - Recall the meaning of this word as it is used in the story. *recall*
C - Give an example of a major event in the story. *give an example*
Ap - What do you predict will happen next? *predict*

Higher Level Questions/Prompts for Reflective Response:
An - Identify relationships between three pairs of characters. *relate*
S - Create a conversation that could have taken place between the
characters in the last chapter. *create*
E - How did you feel about the conclusion of this book? *judge*

Activity
Overview: I Remember When . . . is an opportunity for students to reflect on their
              lives through personal photographs that are brought from home.

Materials: *Looking Back*, by Lois Lowry
              When I Was Little, by Jamie Lee Curtis
              personal photo(s) from home
              student writing journal

Lead In: The teacher might introduce the concept of a photobiography by shar-
              ing the books mentioned above.

Procedure: The teacher will engage students in discussion about reflecting on their
              personal life experiences.
              The teacher will share a picture from an earlier time in life and read a
              personal reflection about it.
              The students will discuss the difference between reflection and
              literal sharing of a picture.

Lower Level Questions/Prompts for Literal Comprehension:
K -   Recall the year that this picture was taken. *recall*
C -   Explain what you are doing in this picture. *explain*
Ap - Demonstrate what you learned from Lois Lowry and Jamie Lee
      Curtis by using your own picture to write a reflection.
      demonstrate

Higher Level Questions/Prompts for Reflective Response:
An - By the expression on your face, can you make inferences about
      how you were feeling that day? *infer*
S -   Reflect on this picture by relating the image to other memories
      you have from that day or time in your life. *relate*
E -   Assess your writing, making sure it is more reflective than literal.
      assess

Activity Overview: Students work in small groups to differentiate among action verbs, helping verbs, and linking verbs.

Materials: article or short story
highlighter or pencil/paper
12" x 18" construction paper
markers, crayons

Lead In: The teacher will present a mini-lesson reviewing action verbs, linking verbs, and helping verbs providing clues for differentiating among the types.

Procedure: Students will be given an article or short story to read individually. As they read, they should underline or highlight all the verbs they find. They will then classify each verb by action, linking, or helping. Students will discuss among themselves the reasons for their classification. Students may design charts that show classifications and rules/hints.

Lower Level Questions/Prompts:
K - What is the definition of a verb? *define*
C - Explain the difference between an action verb, a helping verb, and a linking verb. *explain*
Ap- Can you demonstrate the easiest way to recognize verbs? *demonstrate*

Higher Level Questions/Prompts:
An- Can you list ten verbs from your reading and classify them by action, linking, and helping? *classify*
S - Can you design a chart that shows your peers the difference among the three types of verbs, giving hints and examples? *design*
E - Evaluate which type of verb is the most difficult for you to identify. Why? *judge*

Activity Overview: After a large group mini-lesson, students work in small groups to brainstorm words that have multiple meanings. They will then design a graphic organizer that shows the definition and a picture of each meaning.

Set Up: examples of multiple-meaning words such as duck, bank, wind, and wash
a 12" x 18" piece of construction paper divided into 4 sections for each student
a dictionary for each student

Lead In: The teacher will introduce the concept of multiple meanings and put examples on the board.
The class may look up some words and see how various meanings are numbered in each entry.

Procedure: The students will work in small groups to brainstorm a list of other multiple-meaning words.
Each student will choose one multiple-meaning word, write it on the construction paper, and show a different meaning in each box. If less than 3 meanings, use the last box to write a compound sentence that uses the word in at least two ways.

Lower Level Questions/Prompts:
K - Can you recall some words that have multiple meanings? *recall*
C - Can you summarize what it means to be a multiple-meaning word? *summarize*
Ap- Apply what you know about using a dictionary to help you find more multiple-meaning words. *apply*

Higher Level Questions/Prompts:
An- Given a list of 25 words, can you classify them by single or multiple meaning? *classify*
S- Can you create one sentence using all the meanings of the same word? *create*
E- Can you locate the errors in these multiple meaning sentences? *locate errors*

 **FRISBEE TOSS**

Activity
Overview: Frisbee Toss is a FUN writing/thinking activity in which all students are actively engaged in sharing and processing information and ideas about the book they are reading. A paper plate with student responses written on it is used like a Frisbee.

Materials: paper plate, pens, or pencils for writing

Lead In: Frisbee Toss can be done after a book has been read, after a read-aloud has been completed, or any time you want students to share and process together.
Students should have completed the assigned reading.
Have students sit in a circle, so everyone can make eye contact.

Procedure: The teacher gives a question/prompt with a time limit (you choose).
Students write/draw their responses on the paper plate.
When time is up, the teacher gives a signal, and students must pick up their pencils and gently toss their Frisbee into the center of the circle.
The teacher signals again, and students carefully pick a new Frisbee from the pile in the center of the circle.
This process is repeated until all questions/prompts are completed.
Each round students read what has been written on the Frisbee they have picked up. They respond to the next prompt on that Frisbee.

Lower Level Questions/Prompts for Literal Comprehension:
K - List as many characters from the story as you can in 20 seconds. *recall*
C - Select one character from the list. Generalize by writing one sentence to describe this character's personality. You have two minutes. *generalize*
Ap - Illustrate a scene from the book that includes the character written about on the plate you have now. You have two minutes. *demonstrate*

Higher Level Questions/Prompts for Reflective Response:
An - Who does this character remind you of? Write for two minutes comparing this character to that person. *compare*
S - If you could change one thing about this character's personality, what would it be? Why? *modify*
E - What was the most valuable part of this book? Why? *value*

TALK SHOW (INTERVIEW)

INTERMEDIATE

Activity Overview: This is a role play to better understand a character in the book or an author. Students assume the role of a character or author, while other students assume the role of the talk show host or interviewer.

Materials: copies of a book for each small group (different title per group), desk, several chairs or couch, paper, pencil - costumes and fake microphone are optional

Lead In: Students read the book given to their group and discuss it.
Teacher instructs on character development, descriptive details, and author's purpose.
Students decide which roles they will play in the talk show (either interviewer or interviewee).
Students write a script with good questions and possible responses (have a few different responses for each question)

Procedure: Set up an area in the classroom (or school's theater) like a talk show.
The host/interviewer sits at a desk (with microphone) and the guests (characters or author) sit on chairs or on a couch.
Students go through the script, conducting a realistic interview of the book characters or author.
Talk shows may be videotaped or done live in front of other classes.

Lower Level Questions/Prompts for Literal Comprehension:
K - Name the characters in the story. *remember*
C - Was there a certain purpose for the book? *generalize*
Ap - What would the main character say to our class if he visited? Say a few words to our class as if you were that character. *transfer*

Higher Level Questions/Prompts for Reflective Response:
An - Classify the characters in this book into groups. Explain the groupings. *classify*
S - Design a new book jacket for this book. Which character would you include? *design*
E - Would there be any reason parents would *not* want their children to read this book? *critique/locate errors*

Primary

MATH

Activities

Intermediate

BUYSMART SHOPPER

Activity
Overview: An opportunity for students to practice counting money and making change.

Materials: cash drawer with play money
              objects with price tags
              a student buyer, a student cashier, a human calculator

Lead In: The teacher will present a lesson about counting out money and counting back change.

Procedure: This activity will give students a chance to practice these skills with their peers. They will be pretending to be **BuySmart Shopper** employees, using appropriate social skills with their customers.
              All objects are small and soft that can be tossed and caught by the potential buyer.
              The buyer pays for the object with the exact change or with a larger bill, causing the cashier to count back the change.
              While the buyer and/or cashier are counting orally, a human calculator has written the subtraction problem on the board and is computing the correct answer as a double check.

Lower Level Questions/Prompts:
K -   How much does your item cost? *recall*
C -   What will you say if you are the cashier? *predict*
Ap- Do you have enough money to buy this item? *solve*

Higher Level Questions/Prompts:
An- What is the fewest amount of coins you could pay with? *analyze*
S -   Invent a board game that requires you to count money and make change. *invent*
E -   Which is easier — counting back the change or subtracting the amount spent from the amount you paid? *judge*

 **BAKE SALE**

 PRIMARY

Activity
Overview: As a follow-up to a fractions lesson, students will measure ingredients at home as they bake something to bring to school.

Materials: baked goods brought from home

Lead In: Students will need to check with their parents in advance to do this activity.
              A letter from the teacher will be sent home the week before explaining the cooking activity and its relationship to the math lesson on fractions.

Procedure: Students will review in class the measurement of water in teaspoons, tablespoons, cups, and fractions thereof.
              There will be a discussion in class about possible foods that could easily be cooked or baked at home with the help of a parent.
              The main focus is that the student will read the directions, get the needed supplies and ingredients out in advance, measure the ingredients, and make the dessert.
              These desserts may be sold in the lunchroom. The money may go into the class fund.

Lower Level Questions/Prompts:
K-   What is a fraction? *define*
C-   How many thirds does it take to make a whole? *compute*
Ap- For how much should the desserts sell? *calculate*

Higher Level Questions/Prompts:
An- How can we sort the desserts? What types of desserts do we have to sell? *classify*
S-   What could you add to the brownie to make it more exotic or fun? *modify*
E-   Which person in the class would you name "The Best Cook?" Why? *judge*

 SALT DOUGH PIE

Activity
Overview: Students will use salt dough to make a pie that will be cut into fractions.

Materials: salt dough for each student in a plastic sealed bag
              a piece of wax paper
              a plastic knife for cutting into fractions

Lead In: Students will review what they know about halves, fourths, and eighths.
              Diagrams may be drawn on the board by students.

Procedure: Students will roll their dough into a ball and flatten it on the wax paper into a pie.
              Students will use the plastic knife to cut their pie in halves, then fourths, then eighths.
              The teacher will ask questions throughout the activity to check for understanding.
              Repeat using thirds and sixths.

Lower Level Questions/Prompts:
    K-   What will we make with our dough? *remember*
    C-   Why should we put the dough on the wax paper? *explain*
    Ap-   Demonstrate how you will cut your pie in half. *demonstrate*

Higher Level Questions/Prompts:
    An-   If you cut a pie into fourths, how many pieces are there? *separate*
    S-   If your pie is cut into fourths, and eight people each need a piece, what will you do? *plan*
    E-   How did this activity help you to understand fractions? *assess*

 SPLASH FACTS

Activity Overview: Splash Facts is a colorful poster covered with math facts. It is a fun, artistic, interactive way to practice basic computation.

Materials: poster board per group, markers, paints, crayons, calculators

Lead In: Instruct and provide some practice with various types of computation (basic facts, double-digit computation, etc.)

Procedure: Each group gets one piece of poster board.
The task is to create a "splash" of facts all over the poster board, covering every square inch (do students know what a square inch is?) They must include the answers!
Each member of the group may choose a special color of paint, marker, or crayon to use. This way it is easy to see that everyone participates. (Blue = Jamie, Red = Daniel, etc.)
Encourage students to try higher-level problems
Artistic creativity is encouraged – various fonts, "swirly" numbers, etc.)
When the poster is completely covered in facts, it is time to do a "check/swap." Each small group trades its poster with another group. They use calculators (or their brains!) to check the accuracy of the other poster.
Process this activity using the questions/prompts below.
Display the Splash Facts in the classroom or hallway for all to see. These can be used later for quick fact practice/quizzing.

Lower Level Questions/Prompts:
K- What kinds of math facts are on your poster? *describe*
C- Why do we practice basic facts? *understand*
Ap- Demonstrate how you used a rule for checking your answers. *demonstrate*

Higher Level Questions/Prompts:
An- Compare your poster to the one you checked. Which one included more multiplication or division? *compare*
S- Arrange the posters in order using some set of criteria. *arrange*
E- With which function are we most confident? Least confident? How can you determine that? *evaluate*

CLIMB THE CONE

PRIMARY

Activity
Overview: Students engage in a race to the top of the giant ice cream cone. They progress by passing timed multiplication fact tests each week. Students must correctly solve 30 facts in one minute or less in order to "climb" up to the next scoop on the cone.

Materials: large ice cream cone made from various colors of construction paper; each scoop on the cone is labeled x1, x2, x3, x4, to x12
twelve different math fact quiz sheets (x1, x2, etc.) with facts mixed up; each quiz is cumulative, so the x5 quiz will have x3, x2 and any from the previous quiz
pens or markers for students to sign the scoop

Lead In: Introduce the way Climb the Cone works and the rules for signing your name on the scoop. Provide practice flash cards or other resources for multiplication facts.

Procedure: Once a week, give the Climb the Cone quiz. Each student is working at the level for which they are ready.
Give students 1 minute to complete their quizzes. Collect & grade. Students must have 100% accuracy and all problems completed in order to sign that scoop of the cone and progress to the next level the following week.

Lower Level Questions/Prompts:
K -   How many problems did you get correct? *recognize*
C -   Explain how you solve a basic multiplication problem. What is the algorithm? *explain*
Ap - Use pictures to demonstrate the concept of multiplication. *use*

Higher Level Questions/Prompts:
An - Was there a pattern to your errors? Did you miss the same type of problems or the same exact facts each time? *Recognize structure*
S -   Create a new practice sheet for yourself, including the problems you need to practice before next week's Climb the Cone quiz. *create*
E -   What is the easiest thing about timed tests? What is the hardest thing? *assess*

BRADY'S BURGERS

Activity
Overview: This activity allows students to read a menu, add prices of food items, and use math skills to figure out the total amount for their meal.

Materials: copy of "Brady's Burgers" Menu (or create your own)
             paper, pencils

Lead In: Students have been taught addition with regrouping (or simplify this activity to include only whole dollar amounts to avoid regrouping). Explain that today we will be ordering lunch from Brady's Burgers. Each student must choose food for lunch, and add up the total price.

Procedure: Post the menu on the overhead or enlarge it into a poster.
             Students write down their menu choices on paper, along with the prices.
             Students use addition to figure the total cost for their lunches.

Lower Level Questions/Prompts:
K – What is the cost of a hamburger? What is the cost of an order of fries? *recognize*
C – Explain why restaurants include the price of food on the menus. *explain*
Ap– How much would it cost if you ordered three cheeseburgers? *calculate*

Higher Level Questions/Prompts:
An– What would be the least expensive lunch you could possibly order if you had a sandwich, side, and drink? *break down*
S – Create a menu for your own restaurant. What kind of food would you sell? What would the prices be? *create*
E – Why do restaurants and other businesses often price things at $3.99 instead of $4.00? Or $15.99 instead of $16.00? Why not just round it to the nearest dollar? *evaluate*

BRADY'S BURGERS

Hamburger.....	$2.50
Cheeseburger.....	$3.00
Hot Dog.....	$2.00
Grilled Cheese.....	$2.25
Chicken Leg.....	$1.90
French Fries.....	$1.50
Onion Rings.....	$1.75
Potato Chips....	$ .80
Applesauce.....	$1.25
String Cheese.....	$ .80
Soda Pop.....	$1.00
Lemonade....	$1.00
Iced Tea.....	$1.00
Milk.....	$ .90
Water.....	Free!

Activity Overview: Using a variety of mediums, students work in teams to create original artwork using geometric shapes and solids. Adding labels to the shapes makes this a wonderful instructional display for all!

Materials: food containers (soup cans, boxes, mini-marshmallows, pasta, etc.) glue, paint, markers, index cards (to be cut into pieces and used for labels, fabric, ribbon, and assorted other art supplies – be creative!
one piece of poster board per small group

Lead In: Instruction on basic geometric shapes.
A poster or other bulletin board display in the classroom with the geometric shapes and their names clearly visible to students.

Procedure: Each small group is given their poster board. Have them write their names on the back BEFORE beginning this activity.
Students use a variety of media (textures, fabrics, colors, etc.) to create an original piece of art entirely composed of geometric shapes. Depending on the level of students, you could include geometric solids: cone, pyramid, sphere, and rectangular prism as well.
Students glue objects to the poster board, and continue this process until the group agrees that their "work of art" is complete.
Display the "Shapes Galore" projects for all to enjoy.

Lower Level Questions/Prompts:
K - Find a triangle on your poster (point to it). Find a square. Find a circle. *recognize*
C - What is the difference between a rectangle and a square? What is the difference between a circle and a sphere? *interpret*
Ap- As a group, can you create a square by laying your bodies on the floor? *discover*

Higher Level Questions/Prompts:
An- Count how many of each shape you have in your piece of art. Make a chart to show this information. *compare/break down*
S - What else could you invent using only shapes? *invent*
E - How well did your group work together? Which work of art is your favorite? Why? *critique/judge*

Activity
Overview: Students create an original song about symmetry. They may use a
             familiar tune and change the words, or they may create an original tune.
             At performance time, they must also share at least one example
             of symmetry (drawing, model, etc.) from each member of the group.

Materials: paper, pencil, overhead projector, blank transparency sheet per group,
             overhead marker per group, a variety of musical instruments (optional)

Lead In: Instruct about the concept of symmetry.
             Explain to students that their job is to create a song that will help
             other students remember what symmetry is. They should come up with
             something "catchy" and easy to remember.

Procedure: After the teacher has given directions (see lead in above), students
             work together in small groups to come up with an original song about
             symmetry.
             Each group should write the words to their song on paper.
             Then, they should write the words on the overhead transparency using
             the overhead marker. This will be used when they share their song
             with the class.
             When all groups are ready, they can take turns teaching their song to
             the class, using the overhead to provide text for the class to follow.

Lower Level Questions/Prompts:
K -   Which of these pictures has symmetry? (point to it) *recognize*
C -   In your own words, explain what symmetry is. *rephrase*
Ap-   Find at least 3 objects in the room that have symmetry. Sketch
      them and draw the line of symmetry on each. *apply*

Higher Level Questions/Prompts:
An-   How can you tell if something has symmetry? What tools or
      methods are needed? *recognize structure*
S -   Design a unique figure that has symmetry. Include the line of
      symmetry. *design*
E -   Which figures on this page do not have symmetry? *locate errors*

JUST CHARGE IT!

Activity
Overview: Just Charge It! is a great introductory or follow up lesson about consumer spending.

Materials: one choice card per student
a charge card for each student and $40 cash
a blank one-month calendar and a pencil
calculator optional

Lead In: Ask students how many get an allowance and discuss how this equates to a pay check.
Take a few minutes to discuss with their friends on what they usually spend money.
Students are then given a charge card with a $100 limit and a $10/week allowance for 4 weeks.

Procedure: Each student will have materials on the top of the desk.
A choice card will be given to each student, FACE DOWN.
Each choice card represents one day of the month.
One at a time, a choice card is read to the class.
Each student will make a choice to buy with cash, charge, or say "no."
Responses are recorded on the calendar.
At the end of the month, can students pay their bills?
Interest at 18% (1.5% /month) is added to the balance.

Lower Level Questions/Prompts:
K-   What will you buy? *recall*
C-   How much is your allowance for a month? *compute*
Ap- Keep track of your spending habits on your calendar. *transfer*

Higher Level Questions/Prompts:
An- On what types of things do you usually spend money? *classify*
S-   Plan a monthly budget for your spending. *plan*
E-   Is it fair for consumers to have to pay interest if they have a balance at the end of the month? *judge*

CHOICE CARDS

Pencils on sale! You need some! 10 for $1.00	Bake sale at lunch! cupcakes: 50¢ brownies/cookies: 25¢	Book orders due Friday! Total: $6.00
Yearbooks have arrived! Payment due: $8.00	Video Night $2.00/night or $4.50 per week	Popcorn Day 50¢
Backpack stolen! Replace for $15.00	Chapped Lips lip gloss or chap stick $1.50	Required art supplies! $3.50
Weekly Bus Fare $2.50	Calculator needed for math class $12.00	Allergy medicine needed! pills and nose spray $6.00
Picture Day! Package A for $12.00	Out of notebook paper! $1.50/pkg.	Little League Sign Up! $5.00
Snow Day! Heating bill: $3.00	After School Cheerleading Camp $5.00	Music Downloads 5 for $5.00
After School Pop Sale 50¢ per can	Putt Putt on Saturday $4.00	Haircut $8.00
Video Game Sale! $10.00	Italian Charm Sale! 3 for $5.00	Hair Accessory Sale 5 for $8.00

CROSSWORD COMPUTE!

Activity
Overview: Crossword Compute is an activity in which two students work together
to create a crossword puzzle with numbers as the answers.

Materials: several sheets of scrap paper folded into fourths
a sheet of 1" graph paper for the final product
lined paper for clues
calculator optional

Lead In: This activity can be done as a center or partner activity.
What a fun way to review a chapter, start a new quarter, or end the
week, month, or semester!

Procedure: Students work together or separately to generate four computational
math problems.
Each problem and solution is put on the scrap paper in its own box.
Clues can be problems, definitions, or questions.
Students place solutions on the graph paper, starting with the longest
answers, adjusting problems whose solutions don't connect across or
down.
Moving left to right, starting at the highest line, students number the
answers for across and down clues.
*Demonstrate this in advance. Some may still need individual help.
Label another paper ACROSS / DOWN for clues.
Add more problems if desired.

Lower Level Questions/Prompts: check
K-   What types of problems will you use for this activity? *recall*
C-   What is being asked in this clue? *understand*
Ap-   How did you get the correct answer for each problem? *calculate*

Higher Level Questions/Prompts:
An-   Which problems should go on the graph paper first? *classify*
S-   How will you make sure all problems connect to one another? *plan*
E-   Why are problems with more than two digits easier to work with?
evaluate

GRAPH IT!

PRIMARY or INTERMEDIATE

Activity
Overview: Graph It is an activity that allows students to create their own graphs using M and M's®. This activity can be used to teach or review the concept of creating line graphs, bar graphs, or pictographs.

Materials: 1" graph paper
              20-30 M&M®'s per student
              pencil, fine-tipped marker, ruler

Lead In: The teacher will have modeled for students how to make the various types of graphs.
              Students will also be aware of neatness and planning in advance.

Procedure: Students will use pencils and M&M's® to make their graphs:
              M & M's® to make the bars
              M & M's® at the points connected by lines
              M & M's® as the pictures
              When finished, students may glue them down OR trace them before eating!

Lower Level Questions/Prompts:
K -   What kinds of graphs have we studied? *recall*
C -   Explain how you would set up a bar graph. *explain*
Ap-   Can you show how M&M's® might be used in each type of graph? *demonstrate*

Higher Level Questions/Prompts:
An-   How many M&M's® would represent 25 children on the pictograph? *recognize structure*
S -   If the value of each M&M® changes, how will you revise your graph? *modify*
E -   "M&M's ®melt in your mouth, not in your hands." Is this true? *conclude*

FOOD COURT

Activity
Overview: Food Court is an activity that increases student awareness of the amount of calories in fast food.

Materials: Food Court menu
$5.00

Lead In: Based on 2,000 calories per day, students will determine how many calories they will allot for lunch.
They will then be given $5.00 and a Food Court menu.

Procedure: Students will have three minutes to make their choices from one restaurant only, staying under $5.00.
10% tax should be added to the total.

Lower Level Questions/Prompts:
K-   What kinds of food do you like to eat for lunch? *recall*
C-   Explain how you decided on your number of lunch calories. *explain*
Ap- Which restaurant probably serves food with the lowest calories? *predict*

Higher Level Questions/Prompts:
An- What types of foods make the lowest calorie lunch? *compare*
S-   How might you change what you normally eat for lunch? *modify*
E-   What general conclusion can you make about people who continuously eat at restaurants that serve the highest calorie foods? *conclude*

FOOD COURT MENU

HARRY'S HAMBURGERS

	calories	price
Cheeseburger Deluxe	600	$2.50
Fried Chicken Sandwich	400	$3.00
French Fries	350	$1.50
Milkshake	350	$2.00
Soda	250	$1.00

PACO'S PIZZARIA

	calories	price
Cheese Slice	350	$2.00
Pepperoni Slice	450	$3.00
Cheese Garlic Bread	300	$2.00
Soda	250	$1.50
2% Milk	150	$1.00

SAMMY'S SUBS

	calories	price
Garden Salad/Dressing	350	$2.50
Meatball Sub	450	$3.50
Turkey Sub	350	$3.00
Chips	200	$ .50
Soda	250	$1.50

DEE DEE'S DAIRY DELIGHT

	calories	price
BBQ Beef Sandwich	400	$3.50
Hot Fudge Sundae	350	$3.50
Frozen Yogurt-Lg.	300	$2.50
Milkshake	400	$3.00
2% Milk	150	$1.00

VITO'S VEGGIE STAND

	calories	price
BLT Sandwich	300	$2.50
Ham Salad Sandwich	350	$3.00
Chef Salad	300	$3.00
Dressing	300	$ .50

FRED'S FRESH FRUIT

	calories	price
Egg Salad Sandwich	300	$2.50
Cole Slaw	50	$ .50
Fruit Plate	150	$3.00
Salad Bar	400	$5.00
Fruit Juice	100	$2.00

TAMMY'S TACOS

	calories	price
Nachos Deluxe	650	$4.00
Taco Salad	900	$4.50
Beef Taco	300	$2.00
Chips/Salsa	350	$1.50
Soda	250	$1.00

ROY'S ROAST BEEF

	calories	price
Roast Beef Sandwich	400	$2.00
Grilled Chicken Sandwich	250	$3.00
Baked Potato-Butter	450	$1.50
Roy's Apple Pie	350	$2.50
2% Milk	150	$1.00

Activity
Overview: Students generate questions about the math skills being studied or past skills for review. The aim of the game is to generate a question that the rest of the class cannot answer. Students get points for "stumpers," and the individual or team with the most points at the end of the week, month, or quarter wins! Point totals are posted somewhere in the classroom, which supports skills of data collection, graphing or charting, and adds motivation as this activity is repeated over time.

Materials: paper, pencils, chart for keeping track of points

Lead In: Stump Your Neighbor can be played anytime during any unit of study. Simply explain the aim of the game to students prior to starting. Divide class into teams, small groups, or this can be done individually.

Procedure: Students have up to 5 minutes to generate questions on a given topic. Each group takes turns reading a question aloud to the class. Other groups or individuals try to answer the question.
If the question is answered correctly, the team that answered it gets a point. If nobody can answer it, then the person or group who wrote the question gets 2 points for coming up with a "stumper."
Record point scores on a chart, and continue the game throughout the grading period or year. At the end of the set time frame, the group or student with the highest score wins! Really, everyone wins, because this is a great way to go over information or practice facts!

Lower Level Questions/Prompts:
K - What is the definition of _____? Name a water pollutant. *define/name*
C - In your own words, tell why cities have police departments. *conclude*
Ap - Demonstrate how to correctly add clip art to a WORD® document. *demonstrate*

Higher Level Questions/Prompts:
An - What do these three things have in common: skunk, zebra, raccoon? *connect*
S - Come up with a strategy for reducing the amount of trash we generate. *develop*
E - What is the worst effect of water pollution? Air pollution? *judge*

PIN CARDS

INTERMEDIATE

Activity Overview: This is a cooperative way to work on general number concepts. Students will take turns passing index cards around the room, creating representations for each number.

Materials: 4" x 6" index cards, pencils, thumb tacks or push pin

Lead In: A different, random number is written at the top of each index card.

64	805	1.249

Students may sit in one circle or may stay at their desks and pass the cards around the room from their seats.

Procedure: Each student starts with one card and has 1-minute to represent that number by either a picture or number sentence on the index card.
The student initials the card before passing.
After one minute, the teacher signals that it is time to "pass the pin cards."
Students pass the completed card to the person on their right.
A different idea (representation of the number) is written on the card received. No duplications, please! The student initials the card.
Repeat the passing process three or four times.
Collect all pin cards, have the class sort them into categories, and then pin them to a bulletin board or tape to a wall for display.

Lower Level Questions/Prompts:
K - List five number sentences that represent the number twelve. *list*
C - Accurately solve these basic number sentences. *compute*
Ap - Choose another method to represent a given number. *choose*

Higher Level Questions/Prompts:
An - Separate the representations into categories in some way. *separate*
S - Develop a new way of representing a given number. *develop*
E - Defend your new way of representing a given number. Why does it work? *defend*

Activity
Overview: Students collect data, organize and display it on a circle graph that represents the way they spend 24 hours of their life.

Materials: chart for recording activity during a 24-hour period, poster board, pencil, colored pencils or markers for coloring

Activity:	Amount of Time	Fraction of 24 hrs.	Decimal	Percent	Degrees
Sleeping	8 hours	1/3	.333	33.3%	120
	This is a condensed sample of the chart used.				
Soccer	1 hour	1/24	.042	4.2%	15.12
Totals:					

Set Up: Students will review concepts of collecting and recording data, converting decimals, percents, fractions, and degrees in a circle graph. A letter will be sent home informing parents of this activity.

Procedure: Students collect data over a 24 hour period of time, reflecting their activity.
Be sure to convert the amount of time into a fraction, decimal, % and degree.
Add the total number of hours (must = 24) and total percentages (must = 100)
Construct circle graph using data, divided into properly-sized sectors.
Sectors should be labeled with categories and percentages.
Project must be on poster board, with circle graph, data, name, and date.
Project must be a true representation of a day in the student's life.
Project must be colorful, neat, and may be done using computer technology.
Projects will be shared via oral presentation by each student.

Lower Level Questions/Prompts:
K-   What percentage of time did you spend sleeping? *recognize*
C-   What takes up the most time in your day? *conclude*
Ap - If you spent 7.5 hours at school, what % of the 24 hours would that be? *solve*

Higher Level Questions/Prompts:
An – Why would someone bother to collect and study this data? *identify motives*
S -   Is there a common pattern or trend in how our class spends their time? *discover*
E -   Has this experience been beneficial to you? How? *value*

Activities

ALL ABOUT ME

Activity Overview: **All About Me** is an activity for building inclusion in the classroom. Students display and explain various items that represent themselves. They will bring these to class in an **All About Me Bag**.

Materials: brown grocery bag and 4-5 index cards per student
notebook paper for note-taking

Lead In: Students may decorate the outside of the bag with their names and designs (not pictures of things inside the bag)
Send bags home with instructions to bring 4-5 items back in the bag. Each item should represent something about the child (i.e. a family picture, trophy, favorite toy, etc.) If an item can't fit in the bag, students may instead write the name of the item on an index card. The next day, the class meets to share their **All About Me Bags**.

Procedure: Each student stands in front of the class telling about each item in the bag, using good volume, clarity, and pacing.
Students practice active listening by taking notes about each person who shares.
After everyone has shared, follow up with questions like those below. Have students record responses to the questions in their journals or respond orally with their table group in the classroom.

Lower Level Questions/Prompts:
K - Who in our class has two guinea pigs in their bedroom? *remember*
C - Can someone say in your own words how Josh feels about soccer? *rephrase*
Ap - Use active listening/note-taking skills during our science lesson today. *use*

Higher Level Questions/Prompts:
An - Who has something in common with another person in our class? *connect*
S - If we could create a nickname or motto for our class based on the things we've all shared, what would it be? *compose*
E - In your journal, write the names of the three people who you thought had the most interesting **All About Me Bags** in the class. After their names, write a sentence or two about why they were interesting to you. *judge*

THE GREAT GAMEMAKER

PRIMARY

Activity Overview: Students will create a game board and game questions to enhance knowledge of Social Studies content. Because the questions can be created using your choice information, this activity can go along with any unit of study.

Materials: resources for Social Studies content information (textbook, newspapers, encyclopedias, magazines, books, on-line sources, etc.) templates or game board formats to be used for this activity pencils, pens, markers, crayons, index cards exemplar game (have one made ahead of time as an example)

Lead In: Explain to students that they will each be creating a game of some type. The game should help other kids learn more about the unit they are studying. Have several different types of learning games available for kids to experience, giving them experiences to draw from as they are creating an original game.

Procedure: Students create at least 10 question cards related to the unit. These cards are used in the game.
Students create original games, then play the games with other students in class.

Lower Level Questions/Prompts:
K – What are three questions and answers you are including in your game? *recall*
C – Briefly explain the rules of your game. *explain*
Ap – Demonstrate how to play the game. *demonstrate*

Higher Level Questions/Prompts:
An – Is your game similar to another student's game in the class? How? *compare*
S – Develop a creative name for your game. *develop*
E – Why did you choose that name? *defend*

I'M ME, I'M FREE

PRIMARY

Activity Overview: Students use red, white, and blue papers to cover outlines of their own bodies. On each red, white, and blue paper a word is written that tells something about them.

Materials: large rolls of paper (large enough for students to lay down on and trace the outline of their bodies), markers, red, white, and blue papers (approximately 2" x 3"), glue

Lead In: Discuss the uniqueness of individuals and the need to celebrate diversity. Discus the freedoms we enjoy in the United States and how we should respect and honor individuality.

Procedure: Each student is given several red, white, and blue papers. They write one word on each paper describing something unique about themselves. Students work in pairs to trace their silhouettes and cut out the frames of their bodies on large roll paper.
Students then glue the red, white, and blue papers all over their cutout bodies mosaic style.
When finished, the bodies are covered in red, white, and blue and also reflect the many unique qualities about the individuals they represent.

Lower Level Questions/Prompts:
K - What is something unique about _____? *recognize*
C - What does it mean when we say we have freedom to be ourselves? *interpret*
Ap - Choose one color that best fits your unique personality. *choose*

Higher Level Questions/Prompts:
An – Do you see any common traits on our "free to be me" cut outs? *connect*
S – What do you think we can learn from looking at these cut outs? *hypothesize*
E – What was the best part of this activity? The hardest? *critique*

Activity
Overview: With a purpose of promoting family heritage, this activity engages students in finding out something about their ancestors.

Materials: notebook, pencil, computer, printer, telephone

Lead In: The teacher will have sent home a letter to parents telling them about the study. This will give them time to talk to relatives to find out about their past.

Procedure: Students will draw their family trees, getting information to take them back as far as possible. They may trace the family of one or both parents.

Lower Level Questions/Prompts:
K - What does genealogy mean? *define*
C - What is the main purpose of this activity? *summarize*
Ap- Can you predict how far back you will be able to track your family's history? *predict*

Higher Level Question/Prompts:
An- How will you organize your information? *break down*
S- How will you plan to get additional information? *plan*
E- Ask a grandparent to evaluate your family tree. *locate errors*

 **LONG WAY HOME**

Activity
Overview: In this activity students will make a 3-dimensional map that will show the directions from school to home.

Materials: 24" x 24" size card board, construction paper, glue, markers

Lead In: The teacher will open the discussion by asking students how they get to school. . .by car, bus, or walking.
Give students 5 minutes to write a paragraph that explains how to get home.

Procedure: The teacher will show a neighborhood map with labeled streets and landmarks. Students will see symbols and realize that they take the place of detailed buildings on a map.
With the help of their parents students will draw a map from school to home. The map should show streets, houses, and landmarks. The students will design symbols for their map and create a 3-dimensional map on cardboard that shows where they live in the neighborhood.

Lower Level Questions/Prompts:
K-   What materials will be needed for this project? *recall*
C-   Explain how to get from school to your house. *explain*
Ap- Using your map, demonstrate the fastest way home. *demonstrate*

Higher Level Questions/Prompts:
An- How many streets must you cross in order to get home? *apply*
S-   Create a carpool plan for you and 4 friends or neighbors. *plan*
E-   Why isn't the shortest way always the safest way? *judge*

HAT DAY

Activity
Overview: This is a motivational activity that promotes community helpers and what they do to help everyone.

Materials: hat, poster boards, string, hole punch, markers
guest speakers

Lead In: The class will have been studying about community helpers such as nurses, doctors, dentists, firefighters, police officers, crossing guards, and teachers.

Procedure: Students will choose their favorite community helpers and work alone, with a partner, or in a small group.
They will gather information about the responsibilities of the community helpers chosen. They will make a placard showing how that person helps the community, and they will bring in or design a hat that depicts that person's job. On **Hat Day**, students will wear their hats and placards, and the teacher will invite some community helpers in to visit the classroom.

Lower Level Questions/Prompts:
K-   What are community helpers? *define*
C-   How will you summarize the main responsibility of this person? *summarize*
Ap-   Can you demonstrate a job that this person performs? *demonstrate*

Higher Level Questions/Prompts:
An-   Make a chart that shows what this person's day is like. *clarify*
S-   Write a song or poem about what you plan to be when you get older. *compose*
E-   Which community helper is the most valued? Why? *value*

 **GALLERY WALK**

Activity
Overview: Large papers, covered with content information are hung on the walls
            around the room (or in hallway) like a gallery. Students walk around,
            reading and responding to each gallery item.

Materials: 12" X 18" construction paper, markers, tape, sticky notes

Lead In: Prepare a list of historical facts, names, dates, words, or locations.
            Discuss procedures for how people actually walk around a "gallery."
            This is the procedure they will follow during our "gallery walk."

Procedure: Each student gets a piece of construction paper and a marker.
            Students choose or are assigned topics. Write them boldly at the top.
            Students silently and individually write their ideas about their topics.
            Words, illustrations, quotes, dates, or anything else pertaining to the
            topics may be used. Papers are then taped to the wall in gallery fashion
            (may use hallway if classroom is not conducive to this type of activity).
            Students are then given a small supply of sticky notes, and as they
            systematically walk around the "gallery" of information, they add their
            thoughts, ideas, or illustrations to the signs as they move around,
            using sticky notes for these additions. Allow some time for students
            to reread their papers, with additions. Finally, as a whole group,
            students share the collection of information from their gallery papers.

Lower Level Questions/Prompts:
K – List any facts about the person, place, or event on your sheet.
    remember
C – Summarize why this person, place, or event was significant.
    summarize
Ap – Experiment with different pictures to illustrate your topic.
    experiment

Higher Level Questions/Prompts:
An – Using a Venn Diagram, compare the location on your gallery paper
     to where you live right now. *contrast*
S – Create a "nickname" for your famous person that reflects his/her
    accomplishments or personality. *create*
E – What grade would you give this famous person from history for
    his/her contributions? Why? *judge*

 WHAT WOULD YOU DO?

Activity
Overview: Students gather in small groups to respond to situation cards asking them "What would you do in this situation?" Groups discuss what would be the right thing/wrong thing to do in various situations.

Materials: pre-made situation cards

Lead In: Provide instruction on citizenship or character education.
              Students read literature and discuss the behavior of the characters.
              Did they do the right thing? Should they have done something different?

Procedure: Students are organized into heterogeneous, small groups.
              Each group is given a deck of 10-12 pre-made situation cards.

Sample:
> You find a five dollar bill on the floor of your classroom. What would you do?

Students deal the deck of cards until each card is used.
Students take turns reading and responding to their situation cards.
Variation: One student reads his/her card, then chooses someone else in the group to respond.
Students discuss the right/wrong things to do in various situations.

Lower Level Questions/Prompts:
K – What is good citizenship? *define*
C – Why is it important for people to behave well? *understand*
Ap – Role play a scene from one of the situation cards. *demonstrate*

Higher Level Questions/Prompts:
An – How do adults treat children who make poor choices versus children who choose to do the right thing? *distinguish*
S – Create an agreed upon behavior procedure for our classroom. *create*
E – What should the penalty be for those who are not good citizens? *recommend*

Activity
Overview: Every morning one geography-related question is asked. Students have until the end of the day to find the answer.

Materials: Academic Standards for your grade level
              Knowledge-level questions related to geography (written by the teacher)

Lead In: This is part of the morning routine.
              Students need no prior knowledge to engage in this task.

Procedure: The teacher will have created a **Geography Box** of questions based on the academic standards.
              Each question will be written on a large index card.
              One student will choose a card and read it to the class.
              If it is immediately answered, the activity is over.
              If no one knows the answer, the card is put up on the board until the next morning, giving students a chance to keep looking for the answer.
              The purpose of the activity is to build a knowledge-level content base, freeing students for higher-level thinking activities during class time.

Lower Level Questions/Prompts:
K -   What is an atlas? *define*
C -   How many miles is it from here to New York City? *compute*
Ap- Based on the information in this table, which city do you predict will have the most crime during the next five years? *predict*

Higher Level Questions/Prompts:
An- In what three ways might you categorize the states? *classify*
S -   If you could put our state anywhere in the world, where would it be? *arrange*
E -   Would you rather live on an island or a peninsula? Why? *give an opinion*

Activity
Overview: Students create a series of panels depicting major historical events
              that impacted our lives.

Materials: U.S. history books, notebooks, pencils, 9" x 12" manila paper,
              colored pencils, fine-tipped markers, scotch tape

Lead In: Students will engage in an overview of major events in United
              States History. As each event is introduced by the teacher, a picture
              book will be read, and the event will be placed on a class time line.

Procedure: Students will be given class time for individual or partner reading and
              research. Students will come back together to write a short informa-
              tional paragraph about the topic. Students will then start their drawing
              of the event on manila paper, which has been folded in half like a book.
              Each page will be titled with the event and date at the top, picture in
              the middle (or "under" the writing), and paragraph at the bottom. The
              folded pages will be strung together, accordion style, and taped on the
              back. Students may make a book jacket that ties the project together
              with yarn.

Lower Level Questions/Prompts:
K - When did the *Mayflower* sail? *recall*
C - Summarize the events of the Boston Tea Party. *summarize*
Ap- What prediction about population can be made based on census
     information? *predict*

Higher Level Questions/Prompts:
An- What impact did the Emancipation Proclamation have on slavery?
     identify motives
S - What plan would you propose for making the First Lady's position
     more important? *plan*
E - What event in U.S. history has made the greatest impact on your
     life? *appraise*

Activity
Overview: This activity enhances awareness of the presidents and integrates art with history.

Materials: 2 one-gallon milk jugs per student, papier maché, paint, cotton balls, felt, glue, yarn

Lead In: Students will have engaged in a study of the presidents, with individual students selecting a particular president that they will be studying in depth. Prior to making the actual model of the president's bust, students may find that drawing a portrait is helpful.

Procedure: Students will study the physical characteristics and dress of each of the presidents. They will build the face with wadded up newspaper and masking tape prior to applying 2 to 3 layers of papier maché. Tempra paint, yarn, and cotton are used to finish the face. The "suit" is most easily made with felt that is attached with fabric glue.

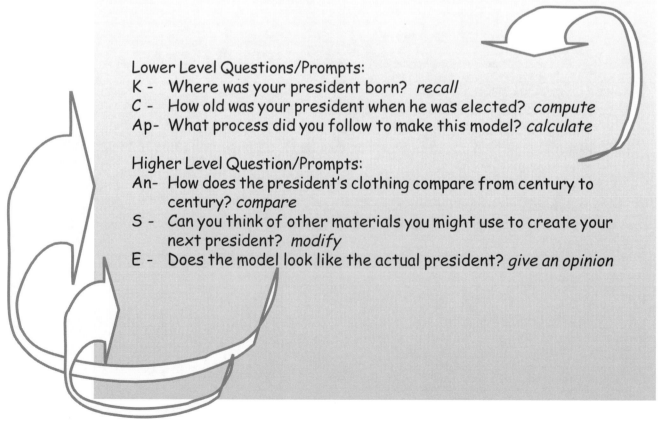

Lower Level Questions/Prompts:
K - Where was your president born? *recall*
C - How old was your president when he was elected? *compute*
Ap- What process did you follow to make this model? *calculate*

Higher Level Question/Prompts:
An- How does the president's clothing compare from century to century? *compare*
S - Can you think of other materials you might use to create your next president? *modify*
E - Does the model look like the actual president? *give an opinion*

TASTE OF EUROPE

INTERMEDIATE

Activity
Overview: This is a cultural lesson that gives students an opportunity to study, prepare, and taste foods from different European countries.

Materials: food from each chosen culture
              note cards

Lead In: Students will be motivated to do this project as part of their geographic and cultural study of Europe. The tasting party may be considered a culminating activity.

Procedure: In their study of Europe, students will collect recipes and ideas for foods that are significant to a specific area. With the help of a parent, they will prepare one of the recipes to bring to class to share. On a specially designated day, students will bring their dishes (along with a decorative table display) for everyone in the class to taste.

Lower Level Questions/Prompts:
K -   Which country is your recipe from? *recall*
C -   Can you translate the European name into English? *translate*
Ap-   Can you demonstrate how you made this recipe? *demonstrate understanding*

Higher Level Questions/Prompts:
An-   How is this recipe different from the way it is typically made in the United States? *distinguish*
S-   How could you use at least half the ingredients to make something entirely new? *create*
E-   Which recipe tastes the best? *critique*

AWESOME ARTIFACTS

INTERMEDIATE

Activity Overview: Students create a 3-dimensional model of an historical artifact. The artifact should represent, authentically, the historical era being studied in the classroom. Students also submit a written report about the artifact.

Materials: various art supplies, paper, index cards for labeling, pens, and colored pencils

Lead In: Teacher provides direct instruction on a historical period.
While students are learning or following the instruction, they choose one artifact that would represent the time period. (ex. Pioneer child's game, Revolutionary War cannon, Roman aqueduct, dinosaur model etc.)

Procedure: Give students the assessment guidelines and time line for this project.
Students create models of artifacts from the historical period.
Students write one-page informational reports about their artifacts.
Final projects are set up like a museum in the classroom.
Students share orally about their artifacts, highlighting the historical relevance as well as any interesting or challenging things they discovered.
Invite other classes and parents to come to your "historical museum" to learn from your students!

Lower Level Questions/Prompts:
K - Name your artifact and what it represents. *define*
C - Describe how your artifact was used and its importance during the historical era it came from. *explain*
Ap- Show the class how the artifact would have been used. *demonstrate*

Higher Level Questions/Prompts:
An- Compare this artifact with a similar object from modern times. What are the similarities/differences? *compare*
S - If you were alive during this historical era, what modifications would you make to this artifact to make it more functional or efficient? *modify*
E - What was the most important thing about this artifact? What difference did it make in history? *judge/assess*

Activity Overview: As an alternative to the traditional (and often boring) state reports, try this approach. Students make a float, banner, wearable sandwich boards, or other exhibit to represent the state about which they are becoming the "expert." An actual parade of the states is held in the school halls.

Materials: (will vary) typical supplies would be: poster board construction paper, tissue paper, markers, and glue

Lead In: Give students requirements, rubric, or assessment tool, and a due date. Send letter to parents and staff explaining the project and date of the parade. Students either choose or are assigned one of the United States on which to focus. Check your State Standards for specific information students *must* know or specific resources they must use.

Procedure: Students work at school and home, researching and creating their parade entries.
When projects are completed, the "Parade of the States" is held. Students carry, wear, or otherwise display their projects as they walk through the halls of the school while patriotic music is playing. Students, staff, and parents line the halls as the parade goes by.

Lower Level Questions/Prompts:
K - Can you name your state, its location, and three facts about it? *remember*
C - In your own words, share what you learned about this state. *summarize*
Ap- Experiment with various types of floats. Which style is best? *experiment*

Higher Level Questions/Prompts:
An - What makes this state different from the rest? What is unique about it? *contrast*
S - If you were planning a trip to this state, what five things would you be sure to include in your trip? *plan*
E - What would be the advantages of living in this state? The disadvantages? *critique*

CURRENT EVENTS ROUNDTABLE

INTERMEDIATE

Activity
Overview: Students gather as a class in a large circle to discuss current events. A designated "roundtable secretary" records comments on chart paper or an overhead.

Materials: current newspaper, magazine, or Internet printout of a current event (local, national, or global), chart paper, markers, overhead

Lead In: Students are assigned the task of finding current events stories, either by reading the local paper, current magazines, watching TV news, or searching on-line. On the day of "roundtable" students come prepared to share their article or information and also to discuss other current events with the group.

Procedure: Students sit in a circle (round table in the middle if you'd like).
Each student shares a brief summary of the event they brought.
Up to two comments or questions are offered for discussion.
The secretary records the events on chart paper, along with key words or comments generated in discussion.
Records can be saved for future reference.

Lower Level Questions/Prompts:
K - What is a "current event?" *define*
C - Which part of the world do you think we will hear about in roundtable today? *predict*
Ap - What resource would you consult to find information on Iraq? *choose*

Higher Level Questions/Prompts:
An - What are the common sections of newspapers? *break down*
S - Design a different format for reporting current events. *design*
E - Why is most current events news focused on negative, violent, or criminal happenings? *evaluate*

MEDIEVAL MOMENTOS

INTERMEDIATE

Activity
Summary: Students assemble a collection of objects that could have been used by medieval boys and girls for various things. The collections are presented and discussed.

Materials: shoebox or other container to hold items, various items from home

Lead In: Students have received instruction on the culture of medieval times. Through literature and other non-fiction sources, students are taught about the remedies used for healing, hygiene practices, weaponry, customs, culture, and day-to-day supplies used in that era.

Procedure: Students are given a certain amount of time to gather objects that represent medieval life in some way.
These collections are shared individually by students, communicating the purpose for each item in the collection.
After sharing, students make labels for each item, indicating its purpose, and the collections are set out on display (possibly in the school library) for all to enjoy.

Lower Level Questions/Prompts:
K – What years in history are considered the medieval times? *remember*
C – Read this passage from old English literature. Translate it into modern day English. *translate*
Ap - Choose one of the following words to describe a medieval girl: cosmetics, dirty, shopping *choose*

Higher Level Questions/Prompts:
An – What were the important sections of a manor? *recognize structure*
S – Design a new outfit for a medieval boy or girl, making sure it would fit with the cultural expectations of the time. *design*
E - Would you have enjoyed living in medieval times? Why or why not? *judge*

Activities

Activity
Overview: Students collect their trash for one day at school. They analyze, measure, and report on their trash, and create a plan for reducing the amount of trash being generated.

Materials: one brown grocery bag per small group, graph paper, pencils

Lead In: Read aloud the book, *Wump World,* to the class.
Provide time for discussion and direct instruction on pollution, recycling, and taking responsibility for the environment.
Tell students they will be working with their table group on a special activity that will help take a closer look at pollution and what they can do about it.

Procedure: On **Brown Bag Day**, place a brown grocery bag next to each table group in the classroom. *Remove the trash cans from the classroom for the day!*
All the trash generated by the table group should be placed in their brown bags.
At the end of the day, analyze the accumulated trash.
Each small group decides how they will sort/analyze their trash.
THE NEXT DAY... Each group graphs their information, draws conclusions, and presents findings to the class.
After all presentations, the class can develop a plan for reducing trash production in the classroom.

Lower Level Questions/Prompts:
K - Which group created the least amount of trash? Which group created the most? *recognize*
C - Explain what we can learn from this activity. *explain*
Ap- Which item(s) do we throw away the most in our classroom? *discover*

Higher Level Questions/Prompts:
An- How much trash could have been recycled? *discriminate*
S - How can people be more responsible for the environment? *create a plan*
E - What is the most important reason to take care of our environment? *defend*

PLANTING POWER!

Activity Overview: In the fall, students plant perennial bulbs in the school yard land-scaping. They do the planning, planting the bulbs, measuring, and caring for the new plants.

Materials: perennial bulbs (be sure bulbs are appropriate for your climate)
trowels, fertilizer, rulers, and gardening gloves (optional)
map of school grounds (birds-eye view)

Lead In: Provide direct instruction on the life cycle of plants as well as the difference between perennials and annuals. Gather many non-fiction books about plants and gardening for your classroom library. Choose various titles for use in reading groups or as read-alouds.
Students go out into yard, observing the layout and current plants. Discuss and reach consensus on the types of flowers and locations to be planted. Consider sun vs. shade. Use maps to mark specific locations. Provide instruction on how to plant bulbs and use tools.

Procedure: Divide students into groups of 3 or 4. This is their planting team. Arrange for parent volunteers to help supervise teams.
In teams, students plant bulbs around the schoolyard.
Place stakes, labeling the bulbs planted in each location, for easy recognition in the spring when plants begin to grow.
Wait all winter.
In the spring, enjoy the perennials, and celebrate the gift of beauty!

Lower Level Questions/Prompts:
K – What materials will you use for this project? *remember*
C – Explain the difference between annual and perennial plants. *explain*
Ap– Draw a step-by-step illustrated "cheat sheet" for planting perennial bulbs. *demonstrate*

Higher Level Questions/Prompts:
An– Why do some bulbs need to be planted deeper or farther apart than others? *recognize structure*
S – Design your own perennial flowerbed. *design*
E – What benefits will our school enjoy because of this project? *value*

THE "WHY" WALK

Activity
Overview: Students go for a 5-10 minute walk to any designated location, practicing the skills of observation and critical thinking. As they walk along, they close their eyes periodically and listen for sounds, learning to observe with more than just their eyes. Students are also encouraged to ask "why" questions along the way. These questions are recorded and brought back to class to discuss and investigate.

Materials: clipboards for each child, paper on which to write questions, pencils

Lead In: Students are taught about observation skills. A list of good "why" questions is created together as a class, integrating the use of the senses to stimulate questioning.
Each child's clipboard should be ready, with paper on which to write and a pencil attached to the clipboard with a string.

Procedure: Students go for a 5-10 minute walk.
They observe the location being visited, and write as many questions as they can in the time given.
Back in class, students meet in small groups to discuss their questions. Each small group chooses the 3 best questions to share with the whole class. Then, the whole class meets to discuss the 3 questions from each group.
At this point, one question can be selected for formal investigation and experimentation by the class. Experimentation follows.

Lower Level Questions/Prompts:
K – What is the punctuation mark used at the end of a question? *recall*
C – Why is it important to observe things closely? *explain*
Ap- Observe one object in our classroom, and ask 3 questions about it. *transfer*

Higher Level Questions/Prompts:
An– Look at your list of questions. Are any of them redundant? *discriminate*
S – How will we find the answer(s) to our question(s)? *plan*
E - What was the most interesting question you've heard today? *give an opinion*

 **SLIGHTLY CLOUDY**

Activity Overview:	This activity integrates science with art. Each group will choose a type of cloud and make a display showing the cloud and giving information about it.
Materials:	18" x 24" blue or gray construction paper, cotton balls, glue fine-tipped black marker
Lead In:	As part of a unit about weather, students will learn about the different types of clouds and the kind of weather they may predict.
Procedure:	Each group will get several cotton balls that will be stretched into the shape of clouds. The teacher should demonstrate this, and each student should try stretching one cotton ball to look like the particular type they are studying. Clouds are placed on the glued construction paper as they would appear in the sky. Students label the type of cloud, followed by its description at the bottom of the paper.

Lower Level Questions/Prompts:
K - What type of cloud are you making? *recognize*
C - Describe what your cloud looks like. *explain*
Ap- Demonstrate how you will stretch the cotton to fit onto the paper. *demonstrate*

Higher Level Questions/Prompts:
An- How is your cloud different from other types of clouds? *contrast*
S - How does the weather affect the types of clouds in the sky? *hypothesize*
E - Which type of cloud is the most beneficial? Why? *judge*

MEAN GREEN GROWING MACHINE

Activity
Overview: As a lab activity during a science unit about plants, students will plant grass seed in a soup can and observe growth patterns.

Materials: empty soup can for each student
soil, water, grass seed, optional plant stimulator
construction paper, glue, markers

Lead In: Students will know that plants need sunlight, air, and water to grow.

Procedure: Students will decide on a character face to put on the side of their cans.
It will be made from construction paper and markers and glued on.
You may need to put rubber bands on the faces while they dry.
Students will fill their cans with soil, plant their seeds, and water.
Students will choose a spot in the room for their plants.
As grass grows, it becomes the character's hair.
Students can chart daily growth.
Characters may need haircuts at the end of the project.

Lower Level Questions/Prompts:
K -   List what you know about grass. *recall*
C -   Why do plants need water? *explain*
Ap- How far down will you place the seeds? *transfer*

Higher Level Questions/Prompts:
An- Why did some grass grow higher than others? *analyze*
S -   What might you do to help your plant grow faster? *plan*
E -   What grade would you give students whose grass did not grow?
Why? *evaluate*

Activity
Overview: One day each week (same day preferred), students will pair up with
a lab partner for hands-on science.

Materials: student pairs
clip boards, pencil, and lab data sheet for each pair
demonstration table
stations set up in advance

Lead In: Students will discuss in advance the type of behavior scientists would
display in a lab.
Materials and procedures will be in place and a lab simulation will be
practiced before the first actual lab.

Procedure: Students will volunteer to bring in lab supplies in advance.
Students will be assigned or will choose partners.
The teacher will explain the directions, possibly demonstrate the task,
and answer questions about the data to be collected.
Students may rotate to several stations or remain at one activity that
is the same for the whole class.
Students will work collaboratively to complete the activity, collect
data, form a hypotheses, and respond to questions on the lab data sheet.
The teacher will ask new questions, rather than answer them, throughout
the activity.

Lower Level Questions/Prompts:
K -   What materials will be needed for this lab activity? *recall*
C -   What is the main purpose for this activity? *summarize*
Ap- Can you demonstrate how you will do this experiment? *demonstrate*

Higher Level Questions/Prompts:
An- Can you diagram your method doing this experiment? *recognize
structure*
S -   Will you write down what you think will happen? *hypothesize*
E -   What general conclusion can you make now that you have completed
the task? *conclude*

 **3-WAY DISPLAY**

Activity
Overview: Each student will choose a subtopic of what is currently being studied in science. With the help of a template, they will design a trifold display of what they learned.

Materials: 3-way science fair board, construction paper, pictures, glue, computer, printer

Lead In: Students will be shown a completed model of a 3-way board that has been done on another subject they are not studying.
The teacher will lead a discussion about neatness, centering, planning space, and displaying important information and drawings/pictures.

Procedure: Students will choose from a list of subtopics within their current unit of study. They will start by reading books and discussing the information they learned with their friends. They will find photos in books and on the Internet, and draw pictures to go with the information they have found. They will use a research graphic organizer to help them organize their information.

Lower Level Questions/Prompts:
K -   What is the title of your project? *recall*
C -   Summarize what you learned in an organized paragraph. *summarize*
Ap-   What illustration did you include to make your project more meaningful? *translate/transform*

Higher Level Questions/Prompts:
An-   Did you simplify your ideas and bullet them? *break down*
S -   Plan a timetable with deadlines for completion. *plan*
E -   Did you think this was a worthwhile project? Why? *judge*

Activity Overview: This activity promotes neighborhood pride. Students will walk through their neighborhoods with parents or caregivers to pick up litter from the curbs or sidewalks.

Materials: a positive attitude, a plastic bag, gloves optional
clip board with data sheet

Lead In: The teacher will lead the class in a discussion about litter and community pride.

Procedure: Students, with the help of parents, will look for a place in their neighborhoods that need to be cleaned up. It might be their own backyards! Working together, they will pick up trash, rake leaves, or do whatever is necessary to make the area more clean and attractive.
As trash is discarded, it should be noted on the clip board. Students should start to formulate categories so that trash could be classified. Findings will be shared the next day.
This is a great newsworthy activity. Call your local paper in advance. They may want to do a story with pictures for the Sunday edition!
Note* Don't go into other people's yards without their permission.

Lower Level Questions/Prompts:
K - What materials will be needed for this lab activity? *remember*
C - What is the main purpose for this activity? *interpret*
Ap- How will you choose the location for the clean up? *apply and choose*

Higher Level Questions/Prompts:
An- How could this activity be a stepping stone for larger, community-wide involvement? *relate*
S - Design a major clean-up plan for your city. *plan and design*
E - Was the project successful? *judge*

Activity Overview: Students will make fossils from plaster and clay.

Materials: plastic objects such as aquarium ferns, shells, spiders, insects, reptile, skeleton bones
modeling clay — not red
plaster mix, water, measuring cup, disposable containers

Lead In: Students will have studied the types of fossils. They will know the difference between mold, cast, trace, and true form fossils. They will have done research about how the different types have formed and where they are most likely to be found in the United States. Great Internet sources for information are: brainpop.com and EnchantedLearning.com

Procedure: This lab will be set up in three stations.
Station 1: Make mold fossils from plastic pieces and clay.
Station 2: Mix your plaster in a half-pint milk container.
Station 3: Pour plaster into your clay mold fossil to create a cast fossil.

Lower Level Questions/Prompts:
K - What are fossils? *define*
C - Follow the directions to make the plaster mixture. *use information*
Ap- Experiment with different types of objects to determine which ones make the best fossils. *experiment and predict*

Higher Level Questions/Prompts:
An- What is the difference between a cast fossil and a mold fossil? *compare*
S - What idea would you propose to make the cast fossils look more aged? *propose*
E - Why did some fossils come out better than others? *judge*

FAR OUT FINDS

Activity Overview: Each Friday, students are invited to bring in any artifact that is related to science. This activity gives students an opportunity to "get up front" and eliminates Show and Tell. They will make an oral presentation that includes an introduction, three new facts, and a conclusion. Students in the audience will take notes.

Materials: scientific artifacts brought in by students
index cards for each participant if needed
a display area for the artifacts
FAR OUT FINDS spiral notebooks for each student

Lead In: Students know that every Friday is **Far Out Finds Day**!
Students will place **FAR OUT FINDS** on a table as they come in.

Procedure: At a designated time during the day, **FAR OUT FIND** presentations will be given.
Students may give their presentations from note cards.
Presentations should be organized and concise.
Presenters should answer audience questions.
Students in the audience will take notes in a **FAR OUT FIND** journal.

Lower Level Questions/Prompts:
K- What is your **FAR OUT FIND**? *recall*
C- Will you summarize what you have learned about it? *summarize*
Ap- Can you give an example of (the type of food this animal might eat)? *give an example*

Higher Level Questions/Prompts:
An- What is one way you could compare your **FAR OUT FIND** to the one that was presented before you? *compare*
S- Can you design a special place to keep this **FAR OUT FIND**? *design*
E- Whose **FAR OUT FIND** was the most interesting today? Why? *judge*

Activity
Overview: One day each week, preferably on the same day, students pair up with a lab partner to engage in scientific experimentation, observation, and data collection.

Materials: various consumables, brought in by students
lab data sheet, prepared by the teacher in advance
clip boards, pencils, timer, optional lab coats
stations set up in advance

Lead In: "This year, as part of our regular science class, you will be participating in lab activities each week. The labs will take place each Thursday. On Monday we will talk about the materials that will be needed for the lab. You may sign up to bring lab materials, and you will earn 5 bonus points for doing this."

Procedure: On Thursday, lab stations will be set up in advance. Data sheets will be attached to clip boards. After a 5-minute overview, students will begin.

Lower Level Questions/Prompts:
K -   What did you sign up to bring to today's lab? *recall*
C -   What is the major concept or theory of this lab? *summarize*
Ap- What diagrams have you included to illustrate your observations? *use (diagrams)*

Higher Level Questions/Prompts:
An- What happens if you skip steps in your experiment? *predict*
S -   What plans will you make with your partner to work more efficiently next week? *plan*
E -   After doing this experiment, what conclusions have you made from your investigations? *conclude*

TRIFOLD DISPLAY

Activity Overview: Students will choose a subtopic of what is currently being studied in science. They will share their research in a trifold display that is integrated with their technological and artistic skills.

Materials: poster board, cut into thirds
construction paper, pictures, typed information
glue, paper cutter, ruler, computer, printer

Lead In: Students will be given an overview of the project at the beginning of the unit. There will be 3 sections:
Left: bulleted information about the topic
Middle: large, centered title in WORD® Art
      pictures, diagrams, photos with captions
Right: research report with at least 5 paragraphs

Procedure: Students will choose a topic from a long list given by the teacher or generated by the class.
Books about the topic will be gathered and class time will be provided for reading, taking notes, researching, discussing, and modeling strategies that yield exemplary projects.

Lower Level Questions/Prompts:
K- Name your project with a centered title. *recall*
C- Summarize your findings in the concluding paragraph. *summarize*
Ap- What illustration will you include to clarify meaning and improve aesthetic value? *translate/transform*

Higher Level Questions/Prompts:
An- Simplify the main ideas in this article, and highlight them using bulleted statements. *break down*
S- How can you rearrange the information in your report to make it easier to understand? *arrange*
E- While doing this project, what have you learned about the importance of organization? *evaluate*

TAKE COVER!

Activity
Overview: Students will learn about safety procedures for dangerous weather
conditions and work with a partner or in a small group to design safety
plans.

Materials: books, pamphlets, Internet, notebook, poster board, construction paper,
markers, colored pencils

Lead In: The teacher will lead a discussion about the importance of safety
during inclement weather. Depending on the locale, students might
plan for disasters such as hurricanes, tornadoes, floods, blizzards,
or earthquakes.

Procedure: Students will get basic information about staying safe from books,
pamphlets, teacher discussion, videos, and guest speakers.
They will choose a disaster or weather condition, design a safety plan,
illustrate their findings on a poster or in a pamphlet format, and
practice it with their classmates. Outstanding submissions might be
shared with the local weather station.

Lower Level Questions/Prompts:
K -   What is a (tornado)? *define*
C -   Explain how a (tornado) causes hazardous conditions. *explain*
Ap- What safety issues will come as a result as this disaster? *infer*

Higher Level Question/Prompts:
An- Compare this type of disaster to others typical of this geographic
area. *compare/contrast*
S -   Design a plan for safety during this type of disaster. *design*
E -   Which type of hazardous weather is the most dangerous?
Why? *judge*

 **BRAIN STORMING**

Activity
Overview: Using guided prompts, students brainstorm as many responses as possible on a given topic. This is a great way to assess for prior knowledge at the beginning of a unit, review information before an assessment, or just stimulate creative thinking.

Materials: overhead projector or white board/chalkboard, markers

Lead In: On the overhead or board, have the word / topic written boldly. Students may work individually or in small groups.

Procedure: Select the topic and announce it to the group. Repeat it – with clarification if necessary.
Allow a one-minute "think time" of silence for students to stockpile ideas. Ask students to respond with one appropriate idea each time they have a turn. Students should not repeat what others have said or skip a turn.
As students give responses, the teacher writes them on the overhead or board. (modeling writing / note taking /abbreviations)
Continue going around the room until all ideas are exhausted.

Lower Level Questions/Prompts:
K - What does it mean to "brainstorm?" *define*
C - How many ideas do you think we can generate on this topic? *predict*
Ap - Use a thesaurus to find other words that could fit with this topic. *use*

Higher Level Questions/Prompts:
An - Can we group the brainstormed responses in any way(s)? *classify*
S - Arrange the responses in a unique way. *arrange*
E - Which response do you dislike or disagree with? Why? *locate errors*

Activity
Overview: Small groups within the classroom work together to come up with innovative proposals for new laws regarding environmental issues that affect them. The class sends at least one proposal to government for consideration.

Materials: pencil & paper

Lead In: Students need prior instruction/exposure to current environmental issues in the news. Have them collect newspaper and magazine articles, Internet stories, and other non-fiction information regarding the environment. Break kids into heterogeneous groups of 3-5 students.

Procedure: Small groups choose environmental issues for this project.
Students gather information about their issues (newspaper, magazine, Internet, phone interviews, etc.) Students draft their innovative proposals for new laws to address the issues. These should be written as business letters to a governmental official or agency.
Each small group presents their proposal to the rest of the class. After all groups have had time to consider the various proposals, the class discusses and selects the "best" one(s) to actually mail to legislators. Perhaps only one proposal will be deemed worthy of mailing, and maybe all of them will. The students can decide. Be sure they give reasons for or against each proposal!
Mail the letter(s) and see what happens!

Lower Level Questions/Prompts:
K- What is the current environmental issue your group researched? *recall*
C- Summarize the problems this issue is causing. *summarize*
Ap- What needs to happen to correct these problems? *predict*

Higher Level Questions/Prompts:
An- What/who are the major contributors to this problem? *analyze*
S - What technology could be invented to assist with your solution/issue. *plan*
E- What is the worst problem being caused by this environmental issue? *assess*

 **WHAT'S IN THERE?**

Activity Overview: Students use creative skills to determine possible uses for unknown objects.

Materials: one large, shiny gift bag filled with various unusual objects or parts of objects, which most students would not recognize
pencil, paper, colored pencils

Lead In: Students have received instruction about simple machines and systems. They should understand that in a system, parts work together to accomplish something.

Procedure: The shiny bag is displayed in front of the class.
A volunteer from the "audience" is called up to pull one item out.
The item is held up and the question is asked, "What is it?"
Students, at their desks, sketch the object, and write as many possible uses as they can.
Popcorn style, students share their ideas. Ideas may be complimented, enhanced, or refuted for obvious fallacies.

Lower Level Questions/Prompts:
K - What are the attributes of this object? *describe*
C - In general, what does it look like? *generalize*
Ap- If we move it into different positions or look at it from another angle, can we learn more about it? Can we see more uses for it? *experiment/discover*

Higher Level Questions/Prompts:
An- If this object was joined with another object, would it be useful? *connect*
S - Create a name for this unknown object. *create*
E - To whom would you recommend this object? Why? *recommend*

CHAPTER 3
CREATIVITY

WHAT IS CREATIVITY?

What do we mean by creativity?

When do we call something creative?

We asked over 100 identified gifted and talented students at the elementary level. Here are some of their insightful responses:

What do we mean by creativity?

Creativity is looking at things from a different perspective. For example: flip it upside down, turn it around, turn it backwards. Amber, age 11

Creativity is the ability to imagine. Marcus, age 11

Creativity is an idea that comes from your imagination. Michelle, age 12

To me, creativity means that somebody is always coming up with new ideas, and are not afraid to express these ideas, even if someone may call it stupid or crazy. Tim, age 10.

Creativity means using whatever materials you have and making something really amazing with it. Kyle, age 11

How do you know if something is creative?

Something is creative it if is unique, out of the ordinary, beautiful, something you don't usually see, your own thing. Megan, age 10

You will know when something is creative when it is "new to the eye." Carmen, age 11

It was excellent, without a flaw, and "thought out of the box." Brodie, age 12

Creative people normally struggle, but if they keep with it they succeed and go far. They normally use the most vivid details and go very far in depth into whatever their idea is. Kyle, age 11

Something is creative when you can tell that someone is using their imagination or their own personal touch. Megan, age 11

You can tell when someone is creative when they always express their own ideas despite what others think of it. Tim, age 10

If someone truly and deeply has an idea, they must express it in a strange or unusual way fitting of the idea. A creative person does not think in the straight and direct line. They take the long and winding trail. A creative trail is the most worthwhile. David, age 12

WHAT MAKES A CREATIVE STUDENT DIFFERENT FROM THE OTHERS?

"The life of the creative man is lead, directed, and controlled by boredom. Avoiding boredom is one of our most important purposes." Saul Steinberg

Creative people . . .

- have a **gift** for combining facts and known information in unusual ways.

- have an **attitude** of openness and flexibility that encourages higher-level thinking — particularly analysis and synthesis.

- **understand** how the creative process works and are **skillful** with each component.

- are **persistent** in their efforts to come up with satisfying results or solutions to problems.

- **search** for solutions by trial and error in a vast array of possibilities.

- **flourish** in a setting where creative thinking is valued and encouraged.

As problem solvers . . .

- their thinking is unconventional.

- they are highly motivated and persistent.

- the problem itself becomes structured by the thinker.

- the product has novelty or value for the thinker.

Creative people ask: "What is the question? What is the question I'm trying to answer, and what would a solution look like, if I had one?" (Simon, p. 52)

HOW DO YOU IDENTIFY
A CREATIVE TEACHER?

According to James P. Downing (1997), there are five basic types of creativity:

Artistic Creativity is a special talent in one of the arts.

While we might automatically think of a creative teacher as one who personally possesses artistic talents, this is not necessarily true. Further, artistically creative teachers must be mindful that their talent doesn't overshadow that of the students, forcing them into passivity as the audience. *Can you take what you know about your own artistic creativity and use it to design lessons and to motivate your students?*

Inventive Creativity is the ability to adapt readily to changing conditions.

This type of creativity meets the demands of complexity and change through flexible, divergent thinking. Can inventive creativity be taught? Yes, by focusing on creative problem solving as well as factual content knowledge. *How often do you give your students opportunities to solve real-life problems?*

Theatrical Creativity contributes a great deal to the level of student motivation and task commitment.

The saying, "Good teaching is 25% preparation and 75% theater (Godwin) holds true not only in relation to student engagement, but also is a major contributing factor to eliminating discipline problems in the classroom. *When is the last time you made a potentially mundane lesson an event?*

Constructive Creativity is really synthesis — the original creation of a new whole where none existed before.

Motivation, opportunity, and understanding the process of divergent thinking all contribute to the creation of new ideas. *Do you value originality and uniqueness in your classroom? Do you allow students the freedom to create?*

Interpersonal Creativity involves the teacher's ability to read the mood of the class on any given day, during any teachable moment.

Have you taken the time to build rapport with each student? Are you aware of how your interaction with students affects their ability to learn and create? In what type of environment does this particular class learn best? Do you encourage students to have a voice?

A creative teacher . . . offers that non-threatening, orderly environment in which students feel free to express themselves. Students make choices about how they wish to express their ideas and mastery of knowledge. Original ideas are encouraged and creative thinking is practiced. A rapport has been established between the teacher and students that lets them know they are cared about and their ideas are valued.

A creative teacher . . . has a gift in the artistic or theatrical arena, but the importance here lies in the way the gift is used to inspire students — not in the degree of the teacher's personal giftedness. Creative teachers present lessons in lively, original formats that engage students.

A creative teacher . . . is playful, open, and willing to take risks while making sure that students are skilled in the process of creative thinking and problem solving. Setting up scenarios that encourage students to communicate, interact, and think is very threatening to many teachers — especially when the outcome of the experience is unknown at the onset of the activity.

A creative teacher . . . lays the groundwork — and then empowers students to take charge of their own learning and thinking. Higher-level questions encourage students to find their own answers. Classroom resources are provided, and questions are presented in a way that make students want to learn more. Creative teachers encourage students to evaluate and reassess as they work, making changes and improvements along the way. They encourage, they motivate, they guide, and they step back.

A creative teacher. . . does not use many worksheets!

TEACHING WITHOUT WORKSHEETS—
IS THIS POSSIBLE?

Can you limit the amount of worksheets in your classroom to one per day? YES! At any grade level? YES! In a self-contained classroom? YES! With multi-age and multiple groups? YES!

We live in a high-tech, interactive world. Away from school, students are engaged in the sights, sounds, and thrills of three-dimensional computer simulations. They carry as many as 1,000 songs in a device no bigger than a credit card. They have access to the Internet and its numerous implications. They can send text messages and pictures through their cellular phones while having a conference call with three other friends. They can activate satellite, cable, DVD player, and surround sound in a matter of seconds. It's no wonder that students die on the vine in classes that have nothing more to offer than read the text and answer the questions at the end of the chapter. How enjoyable is that? How engaging is that? Does it empower students to take charge of their own learning? Society has already laid the groundwork for critical and creative thinking. Why then, do we fail to encourage those skills in the classroom?

Teachers shy away from creativity for several reasons. First of all, their personal creativity may have never been nurtured; they don't see themselves as creative people. Secondly, many teachers feel the pressure to "cover the standards," and in doing so, feel that there isn't time for anything else. Thirdly, there is that group of teachers who have "always done it this way." They have no desire to change and therefore no inclination to learn how. In this chapter, we've attempted to give teachers a clearer picture of what creativity actually is, we've answered a few questions, and given numerous choices for changing a traditional lesson into one that is more creative and thought provoking for students.

If I focus on creativity, how will I fit all the required standards into my day?

The key to "fitting it all in" lies in **curricular integration**. There aren't enough minutes in the day to teach every skill separately. The gift lies in being able to plan effectively, think creatively, integrate intuitively, and motivate constantly. On top of that you need to be highly proficient at asking questions and take advantage of every teachable moment throughout the day. (*Asking Smart Questions* by Frischknecht and Schroeder. Pieces of Learning. 2006)

Can't I just add some creativity to the lessons I have already have planned?

Adding creativity to traditional lessons you have already planned is a great way to get started thinking creatively. Unfortunately, however, many teachers have difficulty thinking of lessons aside from reading the text and answering the questions at the end of the section . . . or doing the workbook page . . . or filling out a worksheet. To help you get started, on the following pages are ideas that will help to make your lessons more creative and appealing to students.

Language Arts

INSTEAD OF THIS. . .	TRY THIS!
a worksheet	write your own sentences
a story summary	draw a comic strip
copying spelling words 3 times	write them once in your best cursive on special paper
8 workbook pages	2 workbook pages that focus on skills that need practice — then add a reflective paragraph to it
matching	fill in the blank or short answer
doing a crossword puzzle	make your own crossword puzzle
choosing the correct definition	write the word and draw the different meanings
using lined paper	use fun paper of various colors, sizes, and shapes
a worksheet	use the worksheet examples for guided instruction at the board
answering 10 comp. questions	reflect on one question
marking answers wrong	model higher-level answers
telling answers	ask questions
giving standard seatwork	set up stations at least once a week
doing everything individually	work in small groups occasionally
copying dictionary pages	make word sort cards
choosing the verb	use the verb on a small poster
practicing the letter parts	write a letter to a friend on fun paper

CLASSROOM SCENARIO

Your students have just finished reading a fiction story in a basal reader or a trade book. As a follow-up activity, you have asked them to write a complete summary of the story — the same activity you did with the last story and the one before that. Instead, why not consider one of the following higher level activities:

ANALYSIS LEVEL

Lesson 1: Turn the novel you have just read into an 8-block comic strip.

SYNTHESIS LEVEL

Lesson 2: Now that you have finished reading the book, are you satisfied with the conclusion? If not, write a new one. Create some new characters, or rewrite one of the chapters with the focus on a different character.

EVALUATION LEVEL

Lesson 3: There's an old saying "Don't judge a book by its cover." How motivating was the cover of this book, and what does the saying really mean?

Math

INSTEAD OF THIS. . .	TRY THIS!
math fact worksheets	work with a partner using flash cards
100 basic fact problems	work with families of facts choose a problem of the day have a minute math warm up
more drill and practice	have short speed contests
playing BINGO	play math fact BINGO
counting change worksheet	count change with money
math worksheets	have students work at the board or on small dry erase boards
marking problems wrong	look for patterns in errors
forging ahead	review and redo in another way
giving more assignments	let students work in groups and discuss
having homework 5 nights	give homework 4 nights
taking a day off of math	use the extra day to concentrate on creative problem solving skills
talking about time	use clocks
talking about place value	use manipulatives to show it

CLASSROOM SCENARIO

You have just completed a math lesson about geometric solids. The objective is to be able to identify them — not only in isolation, but in everyday objects. Instead of fill-in-the-blank worksheets that ask students to identify each solid, you might ask them to try these higher level activities:

ANALYSIS LEVEL

Lesson 1: You have been given a container that contains geometric solids from the math kit and real-life objects that resemble these solids. Sort these objects in at least three different ways. Chart your findings.

SYNTHESIS LEVEL

Lesson 2: You have two choices of what to do with the five basic rectangular solids we have been working with. Create a standing structure that uses the same amount of each solid OR design a pattern for a beaded necklace that uses the solids in multiples of one another.

EVALUATION LEVEL

Lesson 3: Evaluate the importance of one of the geometric solids, supporting your opinion with at least three reasons. Make a poster entitled "Save the _____" illustrating your argument.

Social Studies

INSTEAD OF THIS...	 TRY THIS!
using only the text	bring in lots of related reading material
answering the discussion questions	ask a new question
trying to memorize meaningless dates and events	act them out in comic strip format or as a soap opera script
filling in a time line worksheet	make a time line on a narrow strip of paper
reviewing the whole chapter alone	jigsaw in small groups
just reading about a place	become email penpals
reading about city government	invite the mayor in
learning about local landmarks	create a video about them
current events	report them on a 5-minute daily news show
just studying economics	set up a mini economy or a class business
reading about the election process	have an election
filling in the places on a map	make a map
learning all the historical facts	focus on the important facts and their impact
studying Social Studies in isolation	integrate it with Language Arts and Art
10 comprehension questions	reflect on 3 questions in a letter to the teacher
taking a chapter test all knowledge level questions	create a children's book on the subject include all levels of questions

CLASSROOM SCENARIO

Your class has just finished a unit about the Civil War. Instead of only giving an objective test to measure student learning, consider a higher level, creative project with a differentiated assessment plan:

ANALYSIS LEVEL

Lesson 1: Two armies fought against one another in the Civil War. Show comparisons between the two armies on a chart. Draw each army's flag at the top of its column.

SYNTHESIS LEVEL

Lesson 2: The topic is slavery, and you have two choices. Create a plan for ending slavery or revise the Emancipation Proclamation. OR Learn about The Underground Railroad and design your own detailed slavery escape plan.

EVALUATION LEVEL

Lesson 3: Many battle plans/diagrams are available for you to analyze. By carefully examining them in detail, can you predict the outcome of the battle in advance? Can you judge the effectiveness of each army by looking at the battle plan?

SCIENCE

INSTEAD OF THIS. . .	 TRY THIS!
skipping hands-on activities	focus on science labs
outlining the chapter	outline the chapter with them on the board, a TV infomercial, or in a PowerPoint® slide presentation
using lined paper	use index cards
writing definitions on paper	make word sort cards in a small plastic bag
always focusing on the text	focus on the charts and diagrams
asking questions	let students ask questions
what is	what if
a science worksheet	a science project
writing the data	graph the data
plain paper	a science log book
a small group	a lab partner
a huge science test	smaller science quizzes on half sheets of paper
only reading and discussing	look for related videos
only considering the science text	look for science-related news articles
answering questions	draw a diagram
instead of a worksheet	make a poster
reading about the model	make the model
talking about the moon	observe the moon over 28 days
reading about weather	visit a weather station
telling students to study	show them how to study
collecting multiple worksheets	collect and display art-based projects

118

CLASSROOM SCENARIO

You are in the fourth day of a science unit about plants. Your usual classroom procedure is to assign the pages to be read the night before, discuss them the next day in class, and have students write answers to the textbook questions in complete sentences. Instead of checking for student understanding the same way every day, consider these higher level activities:

ANALYSIS LEVEL

Lesson 1: You have just completed a lab to examine the parts of a plant under a microscope. Draw a diagram, showing the main parts of a plant. Give it a title, color it, and label each part.

SYNTHESIS LEVEL

Lesson 2: We have been talking about the types of environments that are necessary for plants to live. On the board are pictures of six different plants. Choose one and design a terrarium that would ensure this plant's survival.

EVALUATION LEVEL

Lesson 3: Today we will be watching a video about plants. Based on what you have learned during our unit on plants, judge this video. Judgment should be based on interest, accuracy of facts, and inclusion of concepts you feel are important. A rubric will be provided for you, but you will be expected to take detailed notes to support your evaluation.

Chapter 4
Assessment

ASSESSMENT

Testing, Testing, and More Testing...WHAT ARE WE DOING?

Why do so many educators feel negative toward Assessment? During the last decade, America's focus on standardized testing has become quite an obsession.

"American society has embraced standardized testing to an excessive degree." (Zessoules, 48) This quote was published in 1991! And our assessment and evaluation regimen was "relaxed" then compared with today. If 1991 was "excessive," then what word could possibly describe our testing situation today?

The high-stakes tests given in each state influence (or dictate) decisions about institutional goals, teacher performance, and program funding, as well as drive the curriculum and instruction in our classrooms. *This practice must be examined.* We have created a "testing culture" in America. The annual, high-stakes test is a singular act aimed at determining what a student knows at a given time. It is associated with the possession of basic information and skills, but rarely, if ever, delves deeper to assess higher levels of understanding and application.

Interestingly, most of the "big tests" being administered today require highly specialized, yet surprisingly superficial, kinds of knowledge. We test students for what they **know** rather than what they **understand**, and often these kinds of skills have little or no relevance outside the classroom. It is understood that there are "vast differences between ways in which mental work is experienced in school and in real-life settings." (Gordon, 33)

Standardized, norm-referenced tests are simply not enough. We must be *thoughtful* and *intentional* about the types of assessments we are giving and how we are using the data they generate. Assessment must be more meaningful than a pass/fail rating for a school.

So, what is MEANINGFUL ASSESSMENT?

Authentic, meaningful assessment is a far more complex process than simply asking students to regurgitate trivial facts and responses. It is a fuller, more contextual form, integrated closely with what and how we teach the students.

Meaningful assessment includes:
- ⇨ Analyzing ongoing processes of learning
- ⇨ Reflecting
- ⇨ Revising over time

Meaningful assessment causes students to collaborate, converse with others, and take responsibility for their learning. Ultimately, it will amplify their understanding and allow them to apply it in new or surprising contexts. (Zessoules, 52) This is what Bloom clearly outlined in the higher levels of his Taxonomy! This is also what the global work-force *demands* today. Employers want and need workers who can apply their skills in new and challenging situations, not just recite facts and theories. It's about putting skills to the test, with our economic future depending on it. This is one test we can not afford to fail!

In this chapter, we explain and clarify some important misunderstandings about assessing student work. In a simple Question & Answer format, is research-based information and practical insights that will help you get a handle on assessment – both in theory and in practice. We've also included usable examples.

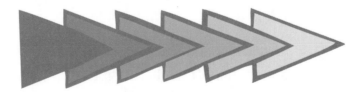

Let's get the "lingo" down...KEY TERMS:

Assessment → Gathering information about students' achievements or behaviors

Evaluation → The process of making judgments about the levels of students' understandings or performances

Measurement → Assigning marks based on an explicit set of rules

Score → The number or letter assigned to an assessment via the process of measurement; the term "mark" is commonly used synonymously with the term "score"

Grades → The number or letter reported at the end of a set period of time as a summary statement of evaluations made of students

WHAT and WHEN do we ASSESS?

We assess students all the time. Each time we observe, share a conversation, or review student work samples, we are assessing in some way.

We are constantly gathering information about:
- ⇨ behavior (how they hold a pencil, how well they focus)
- ⇨ types of questions they ask or answer
- ⇨ performance (did they answer correctly, did they make sense, did they demonstrate creativity, did they show a higher level of understanding)
- ⇨ social skills and interactions
- ⇨ work habits
- ⇨ vocabulary level
- ⇨ ability to communicate skillfully
- ⇨ and more!!!

Not all of these assessments are documented, yet effective teachers intuitively assess and analyze students in an *ongoing* way.

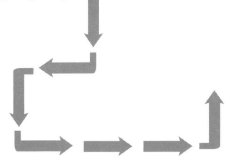

WHY do we ASSESS students?

We assess in an effort to know what students understand and are capable of doing. We assess to maintain an accurate idea of a student's skills and knowledge. We assess to gather data for reporting purposes. We assess to have concrete information which can be used to direct future planning, instruction, and learning. We assess to give students meaningful, timely feedback to enhance and solidify their understandings.

Ultimately, the critical reasons we assess students are:

 to help them *nurture complex understandings*
- ⇨ by assessing and giving feedback on a higher level, teachers can support students as they build complex skills, theories, or ideas.
- ⇨ by letting them know exactly what higher level insights, skills, or understandings they have demonstrated, so they are aware of what they have done.

to help them *develop habits of mind which are both collaborative and reflective*
- ⇨ by giving feedback about how well students work in small groups.
- ⇨ by providing time for students to read, reflect, and discuss the feedback they've been given – possibly setting goals for future improvements.

to *document students' evolving understandings*
- ⇨ by encouraging students to keep track of their evolving skills and assessment results (this can be easily done by recording test scores, teacher comments, and any other feedback in a section of a binder or a file folder).
- ⇨ by celebrating growth.
- ⇨ by setting goals for improvement.
- ⇨ by providing helpful documentation to share with parents.

to make use of *assessment as a learning tool*
- ⇨ by conferencing with students after an assessment, reviewing their strengths and weaknesses.
- ⇨ by allowing students time to ask questions or set goals.
- ⇨ by going over assessment criteria or specific test items, reteaching or clarifying the process as needed.

(Zessoules, 51)

What constitutes "BEST PRACTICE" in the area of ASSESSMENT today?

Good teachers constantly assess how their students are doing, gather evidence of problems and progress, and adjust their instructional plans accordingly. (Herman, 12) The *assessment tools used to achieve this can and should be varied.* As we ask students to perform at the higher levels of Bloom's Taxonomy, to be creative, and to make choices in their own learning, we must, in turn, respond with variety and choice in the way we assess their understanding and the products they submit.

⟫⟫⟫ Assessment **practices** classified as "best practice"

⇨ regardless of format, MUST match the expected outcome (standards) goals.
⇨ allow for the expression of both lower and higher level responses using Bloom's Taxonomy.
⇨ include both holistic and analytic elements.
⇨ document and promote the development of "real world" skills.
⇨ reflect student learning over time.
⇨ build real mastery of a subject or skill.
⇨ require an authentic audience.

⟫⟫⟫ Assessment **tools** classified as "best practice:"

⇨ rubrics (including criteria for content, processing skills, and collaborative effort)
⇨ portfolios
⇨ interviews, oral reports (oral responses)
⇨ checklists, charts, graphic organizers, and graphs
⇨ writing prompts, essays
⇨ performance tasks (real life demonstrations of skill/understanding)
⇨ teacher observations – anecdotal notes
⇨ traditional tests – used in conjunction with other measures

Traditional tests should include a varied format of "forced-choice items:" multiple choice, true/false, matching, short-answer, and fill-in-the-blank. Even short-answer and fill-in-the-blank are considered "forced-choice" because they allow for a single correct answer that is counted either right or wrong. This limits the evaluator from truly knowing what depth of understanding the student has achieved.

Look at the following assessment samples . . .

APOLLO 13 TEST

Name _____ Date _____

DIRECTIONS: Select any combination of questions to total 100 points. As you choose each question, keep a running total of your points in the blanks. Write your answers on a separate piece of paper.

▶ KNOWLEDGE (5 points each)

_____ 1. Define these words: jettison, simulated, odyssey, procedure

_____ 2. Who was the first man to step on the moon? Which Apollo mission did he fly on? What did he say after he stepped on the moon?

_____ 3. Who said, "Catch you on the flip side?" What did he mean? Where does the saying come from?

_____ 4. Describe why the LEM was used as a lifeboat. How did it work?

▶ COMPREHENSION (10 points each)

_____ 1. Explain what Gene Kranz meant by "Failure is not an option."

_____ 2. Explain what Gene Kranz meant by "With all due respect gentlemen, I believe this will be NASA's finest hour."

_____ 3. Give an example that shows NASA is concerned with its public image.

_____ 4. Summarize how the NASA engineers solved the carbon dioxide problem in the LEM.

▶ APPLICATION (15 points each)

_____ 1. Construct a Venn Diagram illustrating the differences between the book and movie.

_____ 2. Compare the public's and NASA's perception of the number 13. Give examples to support your answer.

_____ 3. Predict what would have happened if the explosion occurred after the LEM landed on the moon.

_____ 4. What would be the effects of having a simulated LEM in Houston?

▶ ANALYSIS (20 points each)

_____ 1. Give an example of a simile used in the book. Write an original simile.

_____ 2. Give an example of the three different types of conflict from the book: man vs. man, man vs. self, and man vs. nature. Which type of conflict is more prevalent in the story?

_____ 3. What is the relationship like between Jim Lovell and Fred Haise with Jack Swigert at the beginning of the mission? Why? Does it change at the end of the mission? Why or why not?

_____ 4. Was Apollo 13 a failure or a success? Explain your answer.

▶ SYNTHESIS (25 points each)

_____ 1. Write a letter from one of the following to Jim Lovell during the crisis: Marilyn Lovell, Jeffrey Lovell, Ken Mattingly, or Gene Kranz.

_____ 2. Design a book cover for Apollo 13. Include a picture or design for the cover and a "book flap" description to entice someone to read the book.

_____ 3. Create a six-frame comic strip illustrating a scene from the book.

_____ 4. Write a story to run in the morning edition of an April 14, 1970, newspaper explaining what had happened so far in the Apollo 13 mission.

▶ EVALUATION (25 points each)

_____ 1. Some people view the space program as an important step in scientific development. Others view it as a waste of taxpayers' money. Make a compelling argument for both viewpoints. Support your statements with examples.

_____ 2. List five qualities you think NASA would look for in astronauts. Rank order these qualities from most important to least important. Give 3 to 5 reasons for your first choice.

_____ 3. Rank the following events in order from most interesting to the public to least interesting. What does your list say about human nature?
___ Apollo 8 lunar broadcast
___ Apollo 11 lunar broadcast
___ The breakup of the Beatles
___ Apollo 13 splashdown
___ Apollo 13 flight show
___ Apollo 13 "crisis" coverage

Excerpts from a test created by Karen Ball Jay County, Indiana

Peer Assessment - Checklist

Speech given by _____ Date_____

Speech Title _____

		Yes	No
1.	Did the speaker stay on topic?	___	___
2.	Did the speaker use gestures?	___	___
3.	Did the speaker use enough volume?	___	___
4.	Was the speaker prepared?	___	___
5.	Did the speaker make his/her point clearly?	___	___

Your Name _____

Comments:

Self Assessment – Rating Sheet

Circle the number that best describes you.
(5 = high rating 1 = low rating)

1. I did my project to the best of my ability. (personal best)

    5   4   3   2   1

2. I understand the information included in my project. (learned content)

    5   4   3   2   1

3. I stayed on task and met deadlines. (self-discipline, focus)

    5   4   3   2   1

4. I included all requirements in my project. (complete)

    5   4   3   2   1

_____
Student's signature

1.	2.	3.
Design a rainforest **bookmark**. Include a picture and a message about the rainforest.	**List** 5 trees found in the rainforest. Rank order them beginning with those we should harvest freely and ending with those we should not cut down. Write a **sentence** about each that explains your thinking.	Create a **wordfind** that includes at least 20 words about the rainforest.
(Knowledge)	*(Evaluation)*	*(Knowledge)*
4.	**5.**	**6.**
Working with at least 2 of your classmates who have also chosen this activity, make a **mural** of a rainforest along a wall of your classroom or in the hallway of your school. Show 3 or more plants and animals in each layer of the rainforest.	Create a **poster** advertising reasons to save the rainforest.	Using books and the Internet, research animals and plants found in the rainforest. Find one for every letter of the alphabet. Make an illustrated Rainforest **ABC book**.
(Application)	*(Evaluation)*	*(Comprehension)*
7.	**8.**	**9.**
Read The Great Kapok Tree by Lynne Cherry. Create a **chart** showing fact and fantasy in the book.	Make a rainforest **diorama**. Include all rainforest layers with representative plants and animals in each layer.	Write a **poem** about the rainforest.
(Analysis)	*(Application)*	*(Synthesis)*

I/we chose activities # _____, #_____, and #_____.

Name _____ Date _____ Due date _____

© Pieces of Learning

1. Bookmark	**2. List & Sentences**	**3. Wordfind**
Has a correctly spelled message about the rainforest _____	Lists 5 trees in rank order _____	Has 20 rainforest words _____
Picture shows some aspect of the rainforest _____	Has a sentence about each tree _____	Correct spelling _____
Visually attractive; appropriate shape and size _____	Reasons are logical and are clearly stated _____	Neat and legible _____
Suggested extension: Include title of a rainforest book or website _____	*Suggested extension: Include more than 5 trees* _____	*Suggested extension: Include another paper with definitions of each rainforest word* _____
Possible points = _____	Possible points = _____	Possible points = _____
4. Mural	**5. Poster**	**6. ABC Book**
Shows 3 or more plants and animals in each layer _____	Follows Poster criteria card _____	Has a rainforest plant or animal for every letter _____
Accurate illustration of each layer _____	Reasons are clearly stated _____	Includes name and picture _____
Group cooperation, planning and effort _____	Reasons are logical and backed up by facts _____	Creativity _____
Visually attractive & neat _____	*Suggested extension: Include bibliography of sources attached to poster* _____	Accuracy _____
Suggested extension: Include written explanations and labels _____		*Suggested extension: Include facts about each on each page of book* _____
Possible points = _____	Possible points = _____	Possible points = _____
7. Chart	**8. Diorama**	**9. Poem**
Follows Chart criteria card _____	Follows Diorama criteria card _____	Follows Poem criteria card _____
Clearly shows fact and fantasy _____	Includes all layers _____	Shows knowledge and feelings about the rainforest _____
Accurate information from book _____	Has 2-3 plants and animals for each layer _____	Creative _____
Suggested extension: Compare with another book about the rainforest such as The Lorax _____	*Suggested extension: Include written labels and explanations* _____	*Suggested extension: Illustrate your poem* _____
Possible points = _____	Possible points = _____	Possible points = _____

Points for activities: #_____ = _____ pts., #_____ = _____ pts., #_____ = _____ pts.

Name _____ Total points _____ Grade _____

INDIVIDUAL LESSON PLAN - BLOOM'S TAXONOMY - HIGHER LEVEL

Required Activities Teacher's Choice	Product/Assessment Required	Assessment Required Activities
1. Read background information about how inventions affect everyday life. Take notes as you read.	1. Notes from reading	1. Complete for reading done; accurate; readable
2. Make a time line of the ten most important inventions in your life. Include the date invented, the name of the inventor, and other important facts.	2. Time line	2. Follow Rubric page 107

Optional Student-Parent Cooperative Activity

Student Choices in Ways to Learn	Product/Performance Student Choice	Standards
Application _____ Analysis _____ Synthesis _____ Evaluation _____	Product/Performance Student Choice	Due Date Student Choice

ACTIVITIES - STUDENT CHOICES

Synthesis

5. Design a house that stays cool in the summer and warm in the winter through an alternate energy source.

6. Write a short story that shows changes in life due to inventions that have been invented since 1950.

Evaluation

7. Which invention that you or your family now use could you most easily live without? Write a position paper with five reasons to defend and show how you would live without it.

8. Choose an important inventor. Research his or her life and identify three things that happened that made him or her a good inventor. Give reasons for your answers.

Application

1. Make a model of an invention that would do your homework automatically.

2. List twenty inventions in your house that you or your family use on a daily basis. For each item, list how you would do the invention's functions if you didn't have the invention.

Analysis

3. Make a diagram of any invention. Write an explanation of the functions of each part and how they interact with one another in order for the invention to work properly.

4. Make a list of five inventions that have harmed the environment. For each invention, analyze the types of harm and for each invention, suggest one way the environment could be improved.

CREATIVE WRITING RUBRIC

Name: Date:

CRITERIA		1	2	3	4	5
	Ideas ♦ Relate to topic ♦ Details	♦ Ideas do not relate to topic ♦ No details	♦ Incomplete ideas ♦ Few details to support ideas	♦ Ideas wander from topic ♦ Details support ideas	♦ Ideas relate to the topic ♦ Many details support ideas	♦ Original ideas and extensive details
	Creativity ♦ Creative words ♦ Creative thoughts	♦ Creative words and thoughts not used	♦ Word choice does not evoke images ♦ No creative description	♦ Words used in an appropriate manner ♦ Creative descriptions	♦ Words evoke images ♦ Creative descriptions are used	♦ Words enhance creative thoughts ♦ Elaborate creative descriptions
	Structure ♦ Beginning ♦ Middle ♦ End	♦ Beginning, middle, and end not evident	♦ Weak beginning, middle, AND end	♦ Weak beginning, middle, OR end	♦ Strong beginning, middle, and end	♦ Outstanding beginning, middle, and end
	Mechanics ♦ Sentence structure ♦ Spelling ♦ Punctuation	♦ Poor sentence structure ♦ Excessive spelling and punctuation errors	♦ Sentences unclear ♦ Run-on or fragmented sentences ♦ Serious errors in spelling and/or punctuation	♦ Complete sentences ♦ Errors affect clarity of writing	♦ Complete sentences ♦ Errors do not affect clarity of writing	♦ Complex sentences ♦ Clearly written; easy to understand ♦ No spelling or punctuation errors
Points						
Total points					Grade	

Comments:

from *Solving the Assessment Puzzle* by Carolyn Coil and Dodie Merritt. ©Pieces of Learning

"Oral Presentation" Performance Rubric

Student Name_____ Date _____

CATEGORY	Brando "The Master" (superior)	Hanks "You've Got Skills" (very good)	Stiller "Meet the Speaker" (fair)	Kutcher "Dude, Where's My Notes?" (poor)
Knows the Material	The student knows the content well and has obviously practiced. There is no need for notes, and the speaker speaks with confidence.	The student knows the content pretty well and has probably practiced. May need notes 1-2 times, but the speaker is mostly confident.	The student knows some of the content, but did not appear to have practiced. May need notes 3-4 times, and appears ill-at-ease.	The student could not communicate the content without using notes.
Presentation	The student consistently uses voices, facial expressions, and movements to engage the audience and enhance understanding.	The student uses voices, facial expressions, and movements to engage the audience and enhance understanding several times.	The student tries to use voices, facial expressions, and movements to engage the audience and aid understanding. Some information is left out.	The student does not use voices, facial expressions, or movement. Important information is left out.
Pacing	The student effectively adjusts pacing (slower, faster) to give emphasis throughout the presentation.	The student paces the presentation well, but one or two parts seemed to drag or to be rushed.	The student tries to pace the presentation, but seems to drag or be rushed in several places.	The student tells everything at one pace, failing to change the pace to match the content.
Written Copy	The student submits a neat, well-written, thorough copy of the information included in the presentation.	The student submits a complete copy of the information included in the presentation.	The student submits a neat, but partially incomplete copy of the information included in the presentation.	The student submits a poor quality, incomplete copy of the information included in the presentation.

What TIPS can you share for teachers who use RUBRICS or CHECKLISTS?

 TIP #1: Give students a copy of the rubric or checklist before they begin their assignments.

Being up front with students has many benefits. Most importantly, it sends a message that you care about their successes. You are not packing any surprise punches, trying to trick them into losing points, or getting a wrong answer. You are giving them very clear expectations, along with the point system being used to calculate their grades. By doing this, they should clearly understand the expectations and what they need to do to submit the highest quality products.

After a combined 50+ years in the classroom, we can honestly say that we haven't met a student who comes to school hoping to submit substandard work or get low grades. Sometimes, they simply do not know what they need to do to be successful. Giving the assessment tool (rubric, checklist, portfolio requirements) ahead of time gives students the information, expectations, and point structure they need to know in order to be successful.

TIP #2: Keep the language on the assessment tool kid-friendly.

Teacher jargon and fancy educational terminology can confuse, rather than help, students. The assessment tool should be a tool to support student learning, not a high-level reading challenge that ends up being meaningless or confusing.

TIP #3: Tap into assessment resources.

There are many resources available that have been designed to make creating alternative assessments a painless process. Most states have assessment resources available through their Department of Education websites. Check with your colleagues to see what kinds of rubrics, checklists, or other assessments they have created. Log onto the various assessment websites that are available at the touch of a button.

One website that comes highly recommended is http://rubistar.4teachers.org This website offers a template to make your own rubric in just minutes. Its ready-to-use criteria qualifiers make it handy, and it is quite easy to navigate. Even a beginner can generate a professional quality rubric and print it out within minutes. Check the additional resources on the next page.

http://quizstar.4teachers.org (free quiz maker)
http://www.teachervision.fen.com/page/4521.html (much on rubrics)
http://school.discovery.com/schrockguide/assess.html
http://www.anglit.net/main/portfolio/default.html (portfolios in Language Arts)
http://www.bcps.org/offices/lis/models/tips/assess-elem.html
http://www.educ.state.ak.us/tls/frameworks/mathsci/ms5_2as1.ht
Activities and Assessments for the Differentiated Classroom by Carolyn Coil. Pieces of Learning. Marion IL.
Solving the Assessment Puzzle: Piece by Piece by Carolyn Coil and Dodie Merritt. Pieces of Learning. Marion IL.
Product Tool Bag by Joan Brownlee. Pieces of Learning. Marion IL.
Teaching Tools for the 21st Century by Carolyn Coil. Pieces of Learning. Marion IL.

Do I have to GRADE EVERYTHING?

Absolutely not. However, you do need to assess everything. Excessive grading can create anxiety, which interferes with learning. On the other hand, too little grading can make a course seem too casual or unimportant, leaving students with inadequate feedback about their learning. (Downing, 191) Grading is simply one way of symbolically reporting a student's level of achievement/quality.

Every assignment, project, or task required of students deserves to be assessed. The feedback, redirection, and additional information students receive from being assessed and evaluated are critical to the learning process. If you give students an assignment, and you don't really see the need to grade, assess, or evaluate it, then WHY did you give the assignment in the first place? If you are assigning things as "busy work" then a huge red flag should be waving. This is a true disservice to America's students.

SO, A GOOD RULE OF THUMB IS: IF YOU ASSIGN IT, ASSESS IT!

That does not mean you must grade it. Keep in mind, there are many other effective ways to report on student learning: concretely, visually, orally, and more. Employ a "smorgasbord" approach to assessing and evaluating. Try to include a variety of assessment tools in an effort to give students multiple ways to reflect on and process their learning and their performance.

What are the benefits of ASSESSING using PORTFOLIOS?

Gordon and Bonilla-Bowman report that when students have a solid understanding of the functions of portfolios, they are articulate in expressing their understanding of the concepts and goals of curriculum-embedded assessment. (Gordon, 39)

So, we know that if an educator plans to use portfolios as an assessment tool, it is crucially important to explain the process clearly and in detail so that the students have a highly-developed understanding of the process. (This translates to other forms of assessment as well. Students must be taught about the ways they are being assessed, whether it is via portfolio, essay, rubric, or test. Direct benefits to students are significant.)

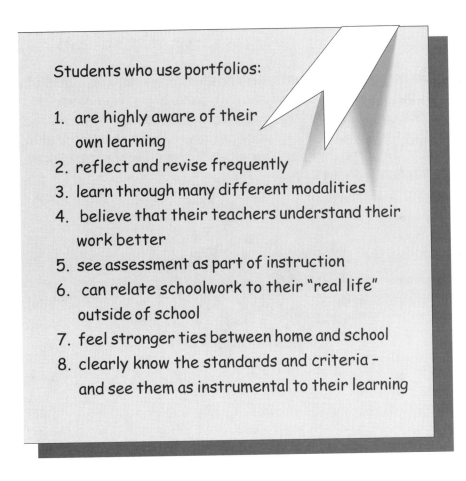

Students who use portfolios:

1. are highly aware of their own learning
2. reflect and revise frequently
3. learn through many different modalities
4. believe that their teachers understand their work better
5. see assessment as part of instruction
6. can relate schoolwork to their "real life" outside of school
7. feel stronger ties between home and school
8. clearly know the standards and criteria – and see them as instrumental to their learning

As students are submitting creative, higher-level products, how should the elements of CREATIVITY be assessed?

James P. Downing suggests that "the creative merit of a student's work should not be graded, although the routine elements and the assignment parameters of the project should be." (Downing, 167) Those routine elements and assignment parameters must be *announced and clarified* beforehand so students understand what they *must* include as they embark on a creative project. Creativity should be encouraged, but not at the expense of meeting the requirements of an assignment.

The "creative flow" cannot serve as an excuse for a student turning in a project out of left field – one which has evolved into something unrecognizable or unrelated to the topic of study. This simply goes along with the fact that in the real world, creative projects (i.e. floor plans, fashion designs, magazine layouts, etc.) must also meet deadlines, formats, and budgets. Learning to work creatively, within boundaries, is a valuable lifelong skill from which students can benefit.

So remember to assess the fundamental requirements of a project, but do not attach a grade or penalty to the creativity aspect. On the next page, you will find a sample assessment for the creative elements of a project. No grades are given, just feedback about the creativity. Grading and feedback for the required elements are handled using a separate document.

Creative Project Assessment

Key: * = yes, you got it!
        ~ = an area that could be improved

_____ 1. Original design and layout were evident in this project.

_____ 2. A unique perspective was included in the presentation.

_____ 3. There was something in this project that no other student thought
        to include: _____

_____ 4. Required elements were included in the project and were not
        "lost" in the creativity.

_____ 5. The content/information was clearly communicated.

_____ 6. Comments from the evaluator: _____

_____

_____

_____

_____

_____

_____

_____

Remember, the bottom line is – a variety of assessment tools should be used. We must measure student learning in a variety of ways, because students can demonstrate their abilities in a variety of ways. Not everyone can demonstrate their level of expertise on a traditional test. Some do better in an interview, while being observed, or by writing their ideas in an essay. Let's not put kids in a box by saying they can only be "competent" if they demonstrate their skills in one way. Let's provide many opportunities for kids to shine.

Abra, Jock. (1988).
Assaulting parnassus: Theoretical views of creativity. Lanham, MD:
University Press of America.

Amabile, Teresa, and Hennessey, Beth. (1988).
The conditions of creativity. Robert J. Sternberg (Ed.), *The nature of
creativity: Contemporary psychological perspectives.* New York: Press
Syndicate of the University of Cambridge.

Anderson, Lorin W. and Sosniak, Lauren A. (Eds). (1994).
Bloom's taxonomy: A forty-year retrospective. Chicago: The National
Society for the Study of Education.

Anderson, Lorin W. and Krathwohl, David R. (2001).
*A taxonomy for learning, teaching, and assessing: A revision of bloom's
taxonomy of educational objectives.* New York: Addison, Wesley,
Longman, Inc.

Baron, Joan Boykoff and Wolf, Dennie Palmer. (1996).
Performance-based student assessment: Challenges and possibilities.
Chicago: The National Society for the Study of Education.

Barnes, Don and Fischer, Wyman. (2005).
Teaching thinking skills using non-fiction narratives. Marion, IL: Pieces
of Learning.

Bloom, Benjamin S. (1956).
Taxonomy of educational objectives, handbook 1: cognitive domain.
White Plains, NY: Longman.

Brescia, Dorothy. (1987).
Creative Crazy. *Challenge: Reaching and teaching the gifted child.* 6,
1-26.

Brownlee, Joan. (2005).
Product tool bag. Marion, IL: Pieces of Learning.

Coil, Carolyn and Merritt, Dodie. (2001).
Solving the assessment puzzle. Marion, IL: Pieces of Learning.

Coil, Carolyn. (2004).
Activities and assessments for the differentiated classroom. Marion, IL:
Pieces of Learning

Davidson, Kay. (2005).
Using bloom's taxonomy to ask over 100 higher-level questions. Marion, IL: Pieces of Learning.

Davidson, Kay. (2004).
You're the teacher. Marion, IL: Pieces of Learning.

Deutsch, Gail. (1985).
Creative problem solving for young people: Aurora, NY: D.O.K. Publishers.

Downing, James P. (1997).
Creative teaching: Ideas to boost student interest. Englewood, Colorado: Teacher Ideas Press.

Feldhusen, John F. and Treffinger, Donald J. (1985).
Creative thinking and problem solving in gifted education, Dubuque, IA: Kendall/Hunt Publishing Co.

Frischknecht, Jacqueline and Schroeder, EllaMarie. (2006)
Asking smart questions. Marion, IL: Pieces of Learning.

Gordon, Edmund W. and Bowman, Carol Bonilla. (1996).
Can performance-based assessments contribute to the achievement of educational equity? *Performance-Based Student Assessment: Challenges and Possibilities*. Chicago: The National Society for the Study of Education.

Gowen, J., Demos, G., and Torrance, E. P. (1967).
Creativity: It's Educational Implications. New York: John Wiley & Sons, Inc.

Herman, Joan L., Aschbacher, Pamela R., and Winters, Lynn. (1992).
A practical guide to alternative assessment. Alexandria, VA: ASCD.

Johnson, Nancy. (1995).
Active questioning. Marion, IL: Pieces of Learning.

Johnson, Nancy. (1999).
The quick question workbook. Marion, IL: Pieces of Learning.

Johnson-Farris, Nancy. (1990).
Questioning makes the difference. Marion, IL: Pieces of Learning.

Lester, John. (2005).
Differentiating lessons using bloom's taxonomy. Marion, IL: Pieces of Learning.

Lytton, Hugh. (1972).
Creativity and education. New York: Schocken Books, Inc.

Maker, C. June. (1982).
Curriculum development for the gifted. Rockville, MD:
Aspen Systems Corporation.

Marzano, Robert J. (2001).
Designing a new taxonomy of educational objectives. Thousand Oaks,
CA: Corwin Press, Inc.

Osborne, A. F. (1953).
Applied imagination. New York: Charles Scribner's Sons.

Simon, Herbert A. (1967).
Creativity: it's educational implications. *Understanding creativity.*
New York: John Wiley and Sons, Inc.

Stanish, Bob. (1988).
*Lessons from the hearthstone traveler: An instructional guide to the
creative thinking processes.* Carthage, IL: Good Apple.

Tardif, Twila, and Sternberg, Robert. (1988).
What do we know about creativity? Robert J. Sternberg (Ed.), *The
nature of creativity: Contemporary psychological perspectives.* New
York: Press Syndicate of the University of Cambridge.

Torrance, E. Paul. (1977).
Creativity in the classroom. Washington, D. C.: NEA Publications.

Torrance, E. Paul. (1970).
Encouraging creativity in the classroom. Dubuque, IA: Wm. C. Brown
Co. Publishers.

Torrance, E. Paul and J. P. (1973).
Is creativity teachable? Bloomington, IN: Phi Delta Kappa Educational
Foundation.

Treffinger, D.J. (1975).
Teaching for self-directed learning: A priority for the gifted and
talented. *The gifted child quarterly, 19,* 46-59.

Zessoules, Rieneke and Gardner, Howard. (1991).
Authentic assessment: Beyond the buzzword. *Expanding student assessment.* Alexandria, VA: ASCD.

Internet Resources

bena.com/ewinters/Bloom.html

businessballs.com/bloomstaxonomyoflearning.htm

cleo.murdoch.edu.au/gen/asset/confs/edtech98/pubs/articles/abcd/delgarno.html

coe.uh.edu/courses/cuin6373/idhistory/bloom_taxonomy.html

coun.uvic.ca/learn/program/hndouts/bloom.html

edtech.clas.pdx.edu/presentations/fvr99/blooms.htm

eecs.usma.edu/cs383.bloom/default.htm

eecs.usma.edu/usma/academic/eecs/instruct/howard/slideshow/sigsce2/index.htm

engin.umich.edu/~cre/probsolv/open/blooms

eprentice.sdsu.edu/J030J/Miles/Bloomtaxonomy(revised)1.htm

faculty.washington.edu/drumme/guides/bloom1.html

first2.org/resources/assessment/Bloom_Taxonomy.htm

gigglepotz.com/miblooms.htm

10n.uillinois.edu/resources/tutorials/assessment/bloomtaxonomy.asp

honolulu.hawaii.edu/intranet/committees/FacDevCom/guidebk/teachtip/questype.htm

humboldt.edu/~tha1/bloomtax.html

kcmetro.cc.mo.us/Longview/ctac/blooms.htm

kent.k12.wa.us/KSD/MA/resources/blooms/blooms.html

kurwongbss.qld.edu.au/thinking/Bloom/Blooms%20planning%20sheet.doc

kurwongbss.qld.edu.au/thinking/Bloom/
Making%20Movements%20with%20Blooms.doc

nerds.unl.edu/pages/presser/sec/articles/blooms.html

nwlink.com/~donclark/hrd/bloom.html

officeport.con/edu/blooms.htm

olemiss.edu/depts./educ_school2/docs/stai_manual/manual8.htm

ops.org/reading/blooms_taxonomy.html

rite.ed.qut.edu.au/oz-teachernet/
index.php?module=ContentExpress&func=display&ceid=29

rubistar4teachers.com

social.chass.ncsu.edu/slatta/hiz16/learning/bloom.htm

stewards.edu/cte/resources/blooms.htm

su.edu/faculty/jcombs/lesson7.20plans/blooms.htm

teachervision.fen.com/page/2172.html?detoured=1

teachers.ash.org/au/researchskills/Dalton.htm

teach-nology.com/worksheets/time_savers/bloom/

teach.valdosta.edu/whuitt/col/cogsys/bloom.html

tecweb.org/eddevel/edtech/blooms.html

umuc.edu/ugp/ewp/bloomtax.html

web.odu.edu/educ/llschult/blooms_taxonomy.htm

webquests.bc.ca/resources.Blooms.htm

web.utc.ac.za/projects/cbe/mcqman/mcqappc.html#C1

wiscinfo.doit.wisc.edu/teaching-academy/Assistance/course/blooms3.htm

wisdomquotes.com/cat_creativity.html